Checker

The All-American Taxi

Checker

The All-American Taxi

Ben Merkel *and* **Joe Fay**

Earlswood Press

First published in 2015 by Earlswood Press, 10 Chaldon Close,
Redhill, Surrey RH1 6SX United Kingdom
www.earlswoodpress.co.uk

British Library Cataloguing-in-Publication Data
A catalogue record for this book is available from the British Library.

ISBN 978-0-9574754-7-2

Typeset by Earlswood Press in Times, 10pt / 12pt

Printed & Bound in India by Imprint Press

Contents

Acknowledgements

Ben Merkel would like to thank those who supplied additional photographs, whose names are listed below. Joe Fay would especially like to thank his wife, Marie for her vigilance in proof reading his original drafts- a vital task for any writer!

Photographic credits

The photographs with no credit given after the caption were taken by, or come from the collection of Ben Merkel. Ben and Joe would also like to thank Byron Babbish, Paul Belanger, Bob Chamberlain, R H Greene, Todd Harroun, Jay Hinkhouse, Erich Lachmann, Tom Merkel, Joe Pollard, Mike Riley, Ken Smith, Lars Wennerqvist and Henry Winningham for contributing to this book.

The publisher would like to thank Olivier Hyafil for the use of his photograph.

Introduction

Many small, independent car companies have come and gone with nary a trace to remember them by. The years pass and the memory of the product line fades with each generation until only a few seniors and automobile experts can recall the brand at all. Checker Motors Corporation, by virtue of its omnipresent taxis in television and movies, isn't one of those wallflowers. The relatively small company may be physically gone, but you can still walk into a gift shop in New York's Times Square and buy a coffee mug or shot glass with a Checker taxi cab on it even though the last, officially-sanctioned Checkers left Manhattan in 1999.

The legend of the Checker is far greater than the car itself for a number of reasons, primarily the 1956 styling that was still available in 1982. Even though Checker was handily outsold every year by other brands of taxi, nostalgic types only have fond memories of Checkers today and all the negative things like leaks, rattles, and rust have been largely erased by time. The unfounded assertion that the cab was built like a tank came from the fact that most people thought they were viewing the same 1956-era taxis decade after decade, but were totally unaware that they were seeing brand new units that just looked old. The distinctive styling is probably the major reason that any Checkers are left at all and I say that by pointing at the pitiful survival rates for its final competitors: it is currently thought that no 1982 Chevrolet Impala, Ford LTD or Plymouth Gran Fury factory-built taxis exist today.

To even compare the Checker to regular production cars is wrongheaded. The cab was built in very limited quantities for commercial use, not unlike a delivery truck, city bus, or postal van. Uneven body gaps, ho-hum assembly quality, and fair paint jobs are all hallmarks of vehicles meant to wear a number and work for a living. They weren't purchased to preen in some suburban garage or strike awe at a highbrow country club. About 500 workers built these cars on an assembly line that dated back to the 1920s and, working together, they only built about 20 to 25 units per day- by hand! It is amazing that such a modest company was able to create such a labour-intensive car and sell it for just a little more than its mass-produced competition. The assembly line itself has been described as a team effort and many ex-employees have fond memories of everybody chipping in when production went down.

Little remains of the Checker legacy today except for pictures, recollections and a dwindling number of actual automobiles. While nobody knows for sure, the number of remaining cars is likely between 1,000 and 3,000. It appears that quite a few of them are still making money as prop cabs and private taxis but many are falling between the cracks because severe use, corrosion, and obsolete parts have made Checker ownership today a challenging proposition.

The purpose of this book is to take a look at Checker Motors and its products in order to gain a better understanding of how the whole thing happened, with an emphasis on the last years. It is certain that the factory never intended to create an iconic cab back in 1952, when finalising the shape of the taxi we know so well today, but it did. By all accounts, and based on their past history of changing whole bodies every couple of years, they should have come out with an entirely new model before 1960 was over. No matter for Checker, though, as 1962 was their best sales year ever using the aged design and I'm sure many would love to see this old-school taxi back in New York City right now.

Ben Merkel
Middlefield Ohio, 2014

1
A Shaky Start

Between 1909 and 1920 three men, William De Schaum, R A Palmer and Charles Darnell successively built an enterprise that would spawn the iconic Checker Cab. In 1921, Morris Markin would take over and run the company until his death in 1970. The original three may have had different visions, motives and goals for the respective cars they produced, but from 1922 Markin would leverage the assets of the once shaky company and put it on a course to become the Checker Cab Manufacturing Company, a large, sustainable automotive manufacturer and global parts supplier. It would continue running for another 90 years.

Like many automobiles of this period, Checker's roots go back further than its original offering in the market. Many have compared the early days of the US automobile industry as being much like the technology boom of the 1990s, such was the rapidity of growth and change. Automotive executives in the early twentieth century regularly switched companies and launched spin-offs and start-ups, and this culture of cross-pollination spread innovative manufacturing and design ideas among the manufacturers. It also established an early pattern of constant bankruptcies, recapitalisation and the discovery of its charlatans.

During this period of expansion, Checker Cab Manufacturing could be traced back to three companies: De Schaum, Partin-Palmer and Commonwealth Motors. William Andrew De Schaum created his first automobile company in 1901. In 1908 *Motor World* Magazine would describe De Schaum as follows: "Mr. De Schaum is a prolific smoker of cigarettes, De Schaum claims to have built a car in 1895 and to have completed in the first automobile race in this country: also claims to have originated the spark plug and several other things of moment." De Schaum introduced his own high wheeler, named "Seven Little Buffaloes", but unfortu-

De Schaum's first offering, named "Seven Little Buffaloes". A simple, high wheeler, it was little more than a motorized buggy. Only 36 units were produced. Although this type of car sold better in rural America, where the roads were often non-existent, by 1909 other manufacturers were producing much more advanced automobiles. (Joe Fay collection)

nately the high wheeler was already falling out of grace in the marketplace when compared to more innovative designs of the day. With only 36 units produced, it was a total failure. Over the course of a year, De Schaum moved about New York State in order to find a place to build his car. He would be wined and dined by Hornell city politicians and businessmen: entertained and enticed to produce his car in their humble city, he settled in Hornell and in 1910 started a new company, the De Schaum-Hornell Motor Company. This venture went nowhere, not even producing a single car. Records show that, after fighting with contractors and business leaders, De Schaum produced conflict and chaos as opposed to autos.

De Schaum left Hornell, never to return. As many young men did back in the early part of the twentieth century, he headed west, to Michigan. He engaged in dialogue with the bigwigs of two Michigan cities: Wyandotte and Encorse, to find a new place to settle and build a new car. Ultimately, settling in Encorse in 1911, De Schaum secured $200,000 in capital from various Encorse investors, personally writing a cheque for $150,000. The new company would make a new car, called the Suburban. Two models were produced: the 4-34, a 20HP two seat roadster and the 28HP 6-36 tourer. Always the promoter, De Schaum had big plans for the new company and secured the mayor of Bad Axe, Michigan to sign on as the President of the company. A 350-acre plot was secured to be developed for manufacturing and a communal automotive village and in 1912 ground was broken for a new factory. Manufacturing was initiated and 10 cars were actually produced, but De Schaum's shady tactics caught up with him and he was uncovered as a fraud. Scandal broke when it was found that the cheque he tendered for $150,000.00 as capitalization was returned

by the bank for insufficient funds. De Schaum was actually broke. He resigned in disgrace on November 12 1912 and died three years later of pneumonia, never to build a car or scam an investor ever again.

In an attempt to save the investors' assets and the company, the board brought in a new leader, R A Palmer, who reorganized the enterprise as the Palmer Motor Car Company. Palmer's first action was to finish De Schaum's partially assembled Suburban cars, using up or liquidating the inventory. Palmer next brought in his own team of experienced car professionals, retaining A C Mason, a known automotive expert who had been largely responsible for production of the first Chevrolet and who had had a hand in the designing of various Buick powertrains. Palmer's next action was to develop a new car, the Model 38, based on one of De Schaum's chassis. Palmer now had a real car company.

To complete the transformation, Palmer found a new partner, the Partin Manufacturing Company. In this partnership, Partin would focus on manufacturing and Palmer on sales and dealer expansion. The growth generated by the partnership allowed manufacturing to move to Chicago and between 1913 and 1915, two smaller cars were added to the product line, the Model 20 and the Model 32. As the company established 400 dealers in their sales network, primarily in the US Midwest it appeared that the car and company was headed for success and by 1915 it was well on its way. This growth required more capital, so the company was recapitalised by bringing in new cash investors, but despite the infusion of money, a lawsuit initiated over a $700 past due creditor bill pushed Partin-Palmer into receivership.

Post-bankruptcy, a new company with a new name was created: The Commonwealth Motor Company. As it was created, the old leadership

Right: the Partin-Palmer Model 20 Roadster was offered with a four-cylinder water-cooled engine of 22 horsepower, including a Gray and Davis generator and optional electric starter. The roadster had a 56-inch track and 96-inch wheelbase. Standard equipment included electric lighting, horn, speedometer, folding top with side curtains, dust boot, speedometer, tool kit and jack, all for US$495. (Joe Fay collection)

team exited and Charles Darnell, the former sales manager was elevated to President. His first task was to save the 400-dealer national sales network. Thankfully, no dealers were lost! Darnell's second focus was to produce 800 cars to ensure the dealer network had something to sell. Upon the creation of the new company, another $100,000 was secured, and with more funds in the bank, Darnell closed a deal with The George D Whitcomb Company of Rochelle, Illinois to produce the automobiles. Whitcomb became Vice President of Commonwealth.

Production was moved to Rochelle and continued into 1916 with the Model 20 and the Model 32, the Model 38 being discontinued.

However, on the horizon was a new model, the Ultra-Four, a higher-end sports model. 1917 was another big year, as the factory was moved to Jolliet, Illinois. The name Palmer-Partin was dropped and all cars were now badged as Commonwealth. Darnell needed to differentiate the new cars from the hundreds of other automobiles sold in the US, so a new slogan was developed; "The Commonwealth, the car with the foundation." This slogan and the associated build concept would in essence establish the Checker for years to come. The 1917 Commonwealth was essentially a modified version of the Palmer-Partin Model 32, but it was designed in a manner consistent with the slogan, with a heavy

Above: the 1918 Ultra-Four Tourer Commonwealth was essentially a modified version of the Palmer-Partin Model 32, with heavy duty chrome nickel alloy steel frame, the top of which was layered with thick felt in order to reduce body squeaks and rattles. Commonwealth developed a European dealer network and the Ultra-Four was put into service globally for taxicab service, including in Germany and the Scandinavian countries. This established a reliable and sturdy path to taxicab production. (Joe Fay collection)

Right: W H Conklin, sales manager for Commonwealth tried to expand the Partin-Palmer network of dealers worldwide. His plan was that secured dealers would buy more inventory and the plant would continue to produce vehicles. The Model 32 depicted in the advertisement would eventually evolve into the Commonwealth Ultra Four. (Joe Fay collection)

A Shaky Start

13

104
POPULAR MECHANICS ADVERTISING SECTION
I have an offer to make you if you will be one of the 300 who are going to profit by being my partners in my new plan
$695.00
COMMONWEALTH
PARTIN-PALMER
34 H.P. — 110 Inch Wheelbase
Five Pass. Touring Car
Demountable Rims
32x3½ Wheels and Tires
Full-Floating Rear Axle
Yacht-Line Body
Only 34 H. P. car selling as low as $695 with so many quality selling features
You can be one of 300 who save money
I want 300 Owner-Boosters in 300 different towns where we have not yet established agencies, to help me advertise this wonderful family touring car. I have a special proposition to make to you and if you will write me quick you can be one of the 300 who are going to profit by being partners with me in my new plan for creating a big market for Partin-Palmer cars in every locality.
Largest, most powerful car for $695
Our regularly established connections would gladly take all the cars we can manufacture this year but I have induced my company to reserve 300 cars in order to make this special proposition to 300 Owner-Boosters in 300 different towns and help me pave the way for a much larger output next season. I have promised my company that each of these 300 cars will sell ten more.
Partin-Palmer cars have made good for four seasons in all parts of the world. Thousands of owners testify today to the value and dependability of Partin-Palmer cars.
The new 1916 Partin-Palmer "32" is a luxurious, comfortable, easy-riding five-passenger touring car of beautiful lines.
In low up-keep cost, in quality of material and workmanship, in all that makes for dependable service, it is the biggest value ever offered.
Dealers:
My attractive exclusive agency proposition will be a money maker for you.
Wire or Write Quick
I will send you by return mail the PROOF that the Partin-Palmer "32" is the greatest buy on earth, and send full details of my money-saving offer to you. So address me personally today.
W. H. CONKLIN, Sales Manager.
COMMONWEALTH MOTORS CO.
Dept. "H," Hearst Bldg.
CHICAGO, ILLINOIS

The Commonwealth Mogul Taxicab was introduced in 1920. Bodies were supplied by The Lomberg Auto Body Company. Although it was built to Commonwealth's specifications, the Mogul looked almost identical to other taxicabs built during the early-to-mid twenties, following the same general outline and configuration. The combination of the Partin-Palmer developed Ultra-Four and the Lomberg Taxicab body would be the start of a taxicab enterprise that would run for the next 62 years. (Joe Fay collection)

duty chrome nickel alloy steel frame, the top of which was layered with thick felt in order to reduce body squeaks and rattles. The resulting platform would be highly desirable for taxicab operators.

In 1918 The Model 20 roadster was dropped and the Model 32 was joined the following year by the Victory Six. In 1920, the Ultra-Four was finally introduced. Far from the sporty touring car promised, it was the old Palmer-Partin Model 32 with a long wheelbase and a Lycoming power plant. But in 1920 Commonwealth was again in financial trouble and required an increase in capitalization. $6m - a lot of money in 1920 - was secured and a major sale was closed between

Commonwealth and a new taxicab syndicate of Chicago, the Checker Cab Company, to produce new taxicabs. The resulting cab was called the Commonwealth Mogul Taxicab. The cab was developed utilizing the Ultra-Four chassis and front clip mated to a wood taxicab body. Final assembly of the Taxicabs was completed by Commonwealth in Jolliet, the vehicles then driven to Chicago for their entry into the Taxicab trade. The body was produced by other body manufacturers. One was a company based out of Jolliet, Illinois, the Markin Body Company, the owner of which would alter drastically the course of the company.

2
Morris Markin Takes Charge

Morris Markin was born in Smolensk, western Russia in 1893. As a young man he was employed in a Russian clothing factory and over a short period of time gained significant experience in clothing manufacture. A hard worker and driven at a young age, Markin soon become a foreman of a trouser factory. Major changes were in store for Russia via a pending revolution, changes that Markin was not interested in participating in, so resisting the political climate, he emigrated to the United States in 1913.

He found work with his uncle as a tailor in Chicago and demonstrated significant business acumen, which ultimately led him to start his own ready-made trousers business. Upon the entry of the USA into the Great War, Markin was contracted by the US Army to produce uniforms for the force fighting in Europe. At war's end, Markin was sitting on a significant amount of money and was ready to invest in a number of Russian-owned businesses located in the Chicagoland area, one of which was The Lomberg Auto Body Manufacturing Company. Founded by fellow Russian immigrant Abe Lomberg, the company manufactured bodies for several Chicago based auto manufacturers, including Commonwealth Motors Corporation. In order to fulfil the order for Mogul taxicab bodies for Commonwealth, Lomberg was forced to seek funds for expansion, which Morris Markin would provide in the form of a $15,000 loan.

Lomberg's largest customer was the financially floundering Commonwealth Motors, and sales of Commonwealth's Mogul taxis were falling far short of expectations. By the end of 1920, Lomberg could no longer keep up his payments, so Markin took over Lomberg. After Markin took over Lomberg Auto Body, he would also take over the Checker Taxi Company of Chicago. By 1920 Morris Markin would be both Commonwealth's largest supplier and customer. When Commonwealth again went into receivership, Markin was able to take over Commonwealth in order to protect both his taxi and body business. Now having control of all three companies, Markin formed Checker Cab Manufacturing. Via a stock offering, Markin generated the funds required to grow the company and clear the balance sheet of debt. Once Markin had put Checker Cab Manufacturing on the course of solvency, it was time to get back to the business of making automobiles, or specifically in the

Starting out as a tailor, Morris Markin would become an automotive industrialist, taking on the captains of the industry and building the longest lasting independent US auto manufacturer (Joe Fay collection)

Above: the Model H. Its similarity with the Commonwealth Mogul on page 14 is clear to see. (Joe Fay collection)

Below: restored by Checker Motors Corporation in the 1960s, this Model H was used for promotional programmes, in this case the Checker booth at the Chicago Auto Show. (chicagoautoshow.com)

case of Checker, taxicabs. In 1922, Checker offered its first taxicab, the Model C, undoubtedly a carbon copy of the Commonwealth Mogul Taxicab introduced two years earlier, which itself was essentially a Partin-Palmer Ultra-Four Model 40.

In May 1923, one of Markin's first major moves was to consolidate manufacturing in Kalamazoo, Michigan, which was developing as a centre of auto manufacturing. Kalamazoo's city fathers were most pleased when Markin acquired the Handley-Knight plant, because unlike the failed brands before them, Checker was proving itself a viable and growing business concern which could absorb some of Kalamazoo's unemployed.

Built in 1920, the Handley-Knight plant was used for final assembly after the bodies had been constructed across town at the 200,000 sq ft, four-storey Dort facility. Markin purchased both, for a price said to be between $2,000,000 and $3,000,000, a tidy sum in those days. Until the Dort property was ready to produce cab bodies, Checker contracted with body companies in Springfield, Massachusetts and Indianapolis, Indiana, including rival taxicab manufacturers Millspaugh & Irish. This company was making a standard body for the taxicab industry, virtually identical to Markin's own. Markin was also able to bring on board Jim Stout and Leonard Goodspeed of another Kalamazoo taxicab manufacturer, Roamer-Barley. Robert Gladfelter of the Dort organization became the plant manager for body assembly. With the Dort plant into its stride, Markin's Checker Cab Manufacturing Company now owned taxicab assembly end to end, with full production capabilities and support of solid experienced manufacturing and engineering talent to grow the business. By 1924, there were nearly 400 workers building about 20 cabs per day, which was still a normal day's production almost 60 years later.

Between 1922 and 1926, Checker would offer "new" models, including the Model H and the Model E. Markin's hype can be attributed to the word "new", as the Model H and E were essentially the Commonwealth Mogul with new model names. Both were offered with a choice of 117- and 127-inch wheelbase and continued to use the Buda four-cylinder engine that Markin had switched to after he started manufacturing under the Checker name. The most significant difference in design appears to be the larger chrome bumpers, compared to the flimsy steel bumpers seen on the Model C. In 1926 an export version of the Model E was offered for the UK market, with right hand drive and opening landaulet rear passenger section. It's highly likely that the two models were produced so Checker could reduce the stock of Model E parts inventory, as the underpinnings of the Model F were still linked back to a ten year old Partin-Palmer design. Based on photographs it appears that the Model F had a slightly altered body with a slanted windshield behind the cowl, a feature that had yet to be offered by any of the major US automotive companies.

A new Model G was offered for 1927 along with the Model F. The Model E, a seven-year-old design was then discontinued. Although both the Model G and Model F still utilized the Partin-Palmer foundation, balloon tyres gave the Model G a new, lower stance. Two new bodies were offered, a limousine sedan and a landaulet taxicab. The four-cylinder Buda engine was again standard equipment, with a six-cylinder Buda engine available with the 127-inch wheelbase.

There were major changes at Checker in 1928 with a truly new model, the Model K. An advanced, modern design for its day, it was now a purpose built taxi with luxurious town car styling cues. The body was integrated in its design bumper to bumper; no longer did it possess the Partin-Palmer front clip mated to a taxicab body. Consistent with previous Checkers, the Model K utilized a 127-inch wheelbase and the Buda six-cylinder was now the only engine available. From its introduction in October, taxicab operators fell in love with the car and orders came piling in. By month's

Above: the 1924 Model F had a slightly altered body compared to the Model H. The slanted windshield behind the cowl was a feature that had yet to be offered by any of the major US automotive companies. Underpinnings of the Model F were still linked back to a ten year old Partin-Palmer design. (Joe Fay collection)

Below: the Model G was offered for 1927 along with the Model F. Balloon tyres gave it a lower, more modern stance compared to previous models. Two new bodies were offered: a limousine sedan and a laundaulet taxicab. Depicted in this picture is a limousine operated by the DeLuxe Cab Co. (Joe Fay collection)

end there were over 4,800 orders. By January 1929, 950 units had been produced and sold. At the end of January, over 8,000 Checkers of all models were chasing fares in New York City, a city with a total population of 21,000 cabs. This made Checker one of the two dominant taxicab builders in the US, the other being Yellow Cab Manufacturing. Together, they pushed the other taxicab producers, Premier, Pennant and HCS out of the market and these two taxicab giants would slug it out through the next decade.

The Model K was offered in two body styles, landaulet and limousine on a 117- or 127-inch wheelbase, although the 117-inch wheelbase was deleted in 1929. The landaulet taxi separated the driver's compartment from an enclosed rear passenger section, making it look very similar to the grand town cars that serviced the rich. After a hard day's work in the office, for a few bits of coin, a New York commuter could hop into a faux luxury car on their way to the train station and ride in splendour! Passengers loved them and so did the taxi operators.

Checker was profitable in 1929, which was quite an accomplishment given that the US had just experienced the Wall Street crash. Markin took his profits and continued to expand, purchasing Yellow Cab of Chicago and the Parmalee Transportation Company, which ensured that there would be future buyers of Checker Cabs in two major markets, Chicago and New York. The transaction also sealed the fate of his number one taxicab competitor, Yellow Cab Manufacturing, formerly owned by John Hertz of Hertz car rental fame, who had sold his manufacturing company to General Motors. Markin's purchase of the Yellow Cab Chicago taxi fleet operation was a major setback for GM, as all future cabs purchased by Chicago Yellow would now be Checkers.

Profits for 1929 were also invested in a new Checker taxicab, the Model M introduced in 1931. A continuation of the town car theme, the Model M was quite a striking vehicle. Visually the car possessed some interesting styling cues,

mainly vertical rectangular headlamps and "sugar scoop" fenders to protect tyres in minor accidents. Additionally, the Model M had rear passenger only running boards, continuing the town car theme. Style wise, the Model M looked at home parked next to Cadillac and Lincoln town cars. The Model M utilized a smaller, 122-inch wheelbase, was powered by the Buda J-216 and was equipped with the first electric taximeter, jointly developed by Checker and Pittsburgh Taximeter Company. Both the Model M and Model K were available in 1931.

Checker also introduced the Model MU6 Utility wagon. Not a taxi, it was best described as a convertible station wagon that allowed for varying seating options, somewhat similar to the MPVs produced today. The Utility Wagon was marketed to travelling salesmen, funeral directors and real estate agents; professionals that may require more passenger capacity to serve their respective customer base.

Though still in the midst of the depression, 1931 was still a profitable year for Checker, but that would change in 1932 as the depression finally caught up with the company and after several profitable years, sales collapsed and Checker started to bleed money, generating losses month after month. So bad was the economy that Checker shut down for several weeks at the tail end of 1932. Despite the losses of 1932 and using minimal funds, Checker was able to introduce a new taxicab for 1933, the Model T. This was a highly modified version of the Model M, and both the Model M and K were dropped in 1933. The Utility Wagon was continued conceptually with a new Model T based car, the Suburban. The new taxicab utilized the new Lycoming GU or GUC 8-cylinder engine, riding on a 122-inch wheelbase. Lycoming of Lewistown, Pennsylvania were an independent engine manufacturer owned by E L Cord, whose growing automotive empire included such iconic brands as Duesenberg, Auburn and of course Cord, who would go on to produce the critically acclaimed Cord 810. In 1933 Checker

Above: *the 1928 Model K appears to be the first truly new Checker. An advanced modern design for its day, it became a purpose built taxi with luxurious town car styling cues. This cab sported a bumper-to-bumper integrated design, no longer possessing the Partin-Palmer front clip mated to a taxicab body.*

Below: *the Checker Cab Manufacturing Company's baseball team, posing with a 1928 Model K in front of the corporate office in Kalamazoo. This building was Checker's home until 2010.*

Above: taxicab operators fell in love with the Model K, with its faux town car style and orders came piling in. It was offered in two body styles, landau and a limousine on a 117- or 127- inch wheelbase. The Buda six cylinder became standard equipment on the 127-inch wheelbase and in 1929 the 117-inch wheelbase was deleted. (Joe Fay collection)

Below: the only hint of heavy duty service would be the steel wheels featured on this attractive 1928 Checker Model K limousine. Riding on lower profile balloon tyres, this sedan would have provided passengers an excellent ride. (Joe Fay collection)

Checker - the All-American Taxi

Above: *the Model M was introduced in 1931. It was quite a striking vehicle, with some interesting styling cues, mainly the vertical rectangular headlamps and sugar scoop fenders. Continuing the town car theme, the Model M had rear passenger-only running boards. (Joe Fay collection)*

Below: *utility magnate Samuel Insull ordered a bulletproof seven-passenger limousine with a landau top on a 1931 Checker Model M chassis. British-born Insull had been an assistant to Thomas Edison and had relocated to Chicago in the twenties, where he built an electric utility empire that was eventually valued at $3 Billion. After the market crash, the value of Insull's once valuable utility network collapsed, and accusations of selling worthless stock earned him death threats. Hence the Checker was ordered so as to protect his family.*

The Model T was a highly modified version of the Model M. Full running boards were added and the hood received five portals inserted in rectangular vents. Round headlights made a return with this model. In the latter part of 1930, Checker Cab Mfg Co became the majority owner of Parmalee. Eventually Markin and his associates would controlled 15 per cent of the New York City market, 58 per cent of the Minneapolis market, 86 per cent of the Chicago market and 100 per cent of the Pittsburgh Market, resulting in the total domination of the US cab industry.

would also produce a brand-engineered version of the Model T, the Auburn Safe-T-Cab, which was sold in limited numbers to the Safe-T-Cab Company in Cleveland, Ohio.

1933 found many auto manufacturers in the midst of significant financial issues. As was the case with De Schaum, Partin-Palmer and Commonwealth over a decade before, Checker now needed to recapitalise. Unfortunately for Markin, via a series of capital transactions, essentially a hostile corporate takeover, the corporate board was reduced in size by a group of investors led by millionaire Pierre S du Pont. The smaller board, which included du Pont voted Markin out of the company and named C A Weymouth as the new president. But Markin had a few tricks up his sleeve. He still maintained some degree of ownership and held options to acquire a majority share of the company. Within ten days, he secured the required funds from E L

Cord to take back his company.

With funds secured, new ownership in place and an alliance with E L Cord, Markin got back to the business of building taxicabs. The Model T and Suburban were produced for the remainder of 1933 and well into 1934. In 1934, Checker began development of a new taxicab, the Model Y. It was the third offering in the evolution of the 1928 Model K and quite striking in appearance, with many style cues reminiscent of its corporate cousin, the Auburn, albeit an industrial version. The Model Y also served as a platform for many new Checker concepts to be utilized for the next 50 years. The long wheelbase version could be purchased in 6- and 8-door variations and also offered with an integrated body trunk, a first in the automotive industry. This configuration yielded the first mass produced car with a three box design, years ahead of Studebaker's and Ford's post-war offerings. Other features

Checker - the All-American Taxi

Above: *the 1934 Model Y was the third offering in the evolution of the 1928 Model K. It was an attractive, albeit an industrial taxicab version of its corporate cousin the Auburn and utilized many of the style cues. This Model Y is a New York City cab operated by Yellow Cab. Paint scheme was yellow with a black roof and red stripe. (Joe Fay collection)*

Below: *the Model Y's integrated trunk was a first in the automotive industry. This configuration yielded the first mass produced car with a three box design, years ahead of Studebaker's and Ford's post-war offerings. This example was still serving Checker's New York Parmalee transportation company post Second World War. (Joe Fay collection)*

included a multi-position adjustable driver seat and glass windows in the roof that tourists would love when sightseeing in major cities. Looks alone were not the only similarities to Auburn; the Model Y utilized the Lycoming 148bhp in line GFD 8, the same engine used in the Auburn 850, although later in 1936 there was the option of a 6-cylinder Continental engine. The Model Y would be produced until 1940.

Major scandal erupted in 1936 when E L Cord faced charges of stock manipulation. These charges were linked to the transaction that saved Morris Markin's company from the hostile du Pont takeover. These, along with charges of major shifts in stock value attracted the atten-tion of Securities & Exchange Commission investigators. The action was swift and ripped apart the empire Cord had created. Markin and Cord denied any wrongdoing, but a Federal court order was issued enjoining Cord and Markin from "further violation" of SEC anti-manipulation provisions in their dealings with Cord company securities. The order also simul-taneously announced the sale of Markin's entire holdings in the Cord Corporation to a Manhat-tan banking group for $2,000,000. Via the court order, Markin was able to buy back his company. Checker Cab Manufacturing was independent again and from 1937, Markin would lead the company until his death in 1970.

3
The Model A: a Defining Vehicle

An early artist's depiction of the six-door version proposed Model A, introduced in late 1939. Note the cabin design is very close to that of the Model A that was ultimately produced, sans the closed rear roof. Significant changes were made to the front lip design shown in this artist rendition. (Joe Fay collection)

The 1940 Checker Model A was a watershed taxi, perhaps one of the most significant taxis Checker ever produced,as it served as the basis of all Checkers until the end of automobile production in 1982, with all Checkers subsequent to the Model A sharing its basic underpinnings. The popular Model A11 taxi is a direct design descendant. The most notable feature of the Model A is the steel chassis. This would be modified over the years, but the basic frame would continue till the end of production in the 1980s.

When the Model A was introduced in 1939 it had more interior room than any previous model produced. It was also the first Checker to migrate away from the limousine concept with its driver dividers, focussing on the taxi commodity business: indeed in the Model A brochure, significant emphasis is made that taxi operators should consider themselves the seller of a commodity and should think of new ways to attract customers.

On the Model A, Checker incorporated new features to enhance the taxi passenger riding experience, including the new landaulet top, where at a touch of a finger, the driver could lower the back section of the roof so that passengers could ride in an open-air mode. If shade was required, a cloth awning could be inserted to reduce the effects of the sun, yet still maintain the open-air feel. Passengers in the jump seats were not left out of the experience, because

Above: the Model A as produced. The flat front sugar scoop fenders are clear to see from the side, as is the steel landaulet roof. (Joe Fay collection)

Below: cab 815, operated by a member driver of the Independent Taxicab Operators Association in Boston. Ready for a beautiful summer day, passengers would surely enjoy the open-air experience of the optional canopy. It is finished in ITOA's livery paint scheme of black body, red roof and gold striping. (Joe Fay collection)

above their heads was a ventilated glass roof that passengers could open to increase the flow of fresh air, yet still sightsee through the glass roof. Both the glass roof and the landaulet roof were Checker exclusive features, patented in 1936 and 1939 respectively.

The taxi driver also rode with the comfort of Checker exclusive features. Checker claimed that the seat could be adjusted in no less than 15 positions, because the company had always maintained that a comfortable seat would allow the driver to drive longer shifts and yield greater profits for taxicab operators. This Checker exclusive had been patented in 1931. Above the driver's head was a vent in the roof to allow fresh air to flow into the driver compartment. The driver compartment was now protected during all four seasons and for the first time was heated. Gone were the days of drivers being exposed to the weather. The manual transmission shift was moved to the steering column, again in an effort to improve the overall driving experience.

The rear of the Model A has the very tasteful streamline styling that was very popular at the time. That said, the Model A front end has always garnered strong opinions from automobile fans. Early artist renditions of the Model A depict an integrated streamline design from fore to aft, but the production car sports a very unique, even Gothic front clip. It's unclear why the major change in the front end styling was made to the production vehicle, but it has been said that the "sugar scoop" fenders, inherited in part from the preceding Model Y were purpose built to provide safety from tire damage in minor city traffic accidents. At the time, other taxis with streamlined fenders ran the risk of having a tyre pierced in a minor accident, whereas the Model A had a higher probability of driving away. Some may find the headlights, centred into a Checker shield, ugly, but they also appear to be a way for Checker to integrate their branded logo as an integral part of the overall taxi design. Checker offered an unlimited colour combinations option, and the common belief is

that with the unique front end and spectacular colour combinations, a person trying to hail a cab kerbside could easily identify the Model A Checker and a potential ride.

The Checker Model A was only made for one full year; 1940. 1941 was a shortened model run due to the Second World War. Over the years the rumour grew up that Morris Markin melted down all the body tools and dies for the war effort. Automobile production ceased during the fight against Adolph Hitler and the Japanese. During this period, Checker participated in the fight by supplying the army with trailers to be used with that new invention of the war, the Jeep.

As the war ended, Checker was facing the challenge of designing and producing a new post war car. During this period Checker utilized two innovative consultants, Herbert J Snow and Ray Dietrich. Snow was formerly the chief of engineering at Auburn-Cord-Duesenberg. While at A-C-D, Snow was the engineering leader who designed the front wheel drive system used on the classic Cord 810. Morris Markin hired Ray Dietrich as a consultant in May 1938, for the hefty sum of one hundred dollars a day. Like Snow, Dietrich was an experienced designer, having worked for Briggs, Lincoln, Le Baron and eventually Chrysler. Dietrich's rise at Chrysler was largely based on his redesign of the Chrysler Airflow, with his resulting Airstreams saving Chrysler from the sales failure of the Airflow.

Now, with two of the automotive industry's top engineers, Checker set out to introduce a replacement for the Model A. Called the Model C, the new, very unconventional Checker was to be very different from Checkers of the past, or for that matter any US produced car. Snow's proposal would be a rear engine/rear drive vehicle, much like the Volkswagen Microbus of the 1950s. In a memo in May 1945 Snow laid out his vision. He wrote:

'The primary purpose of a vehicle of this kind is to carry passengers comfortably and economically. To do this, passengers must be placed in the most advantageous seating and riding position.

Above: *On April 9 1940,* The Chicago Sun Times *wrote: "a streamlined taxicab of the type soon to be put into service has been placed on display at the Hotel Sherman. The cab is equipped with portholes, one above the driver and the other over the passenger compartment. The new vehicles are to replace 1,200 cabs now operated by the Yellow Cab Company. The Checker Taxi Company also plans to use this new type of cab." (The Chicago Sun Times)*

Below: *by the end of the Second World War, most Checker Model As had seen over five years of heavy service. This New York City Parmalee taxicab, owned by Checker Cab Manufacturing was pretty beat up. Parmalee's Paint Scheme was a green body trimmed in checkerboard with white roof and fenders. (Joe Fay collection)*

The Model C test mule utilized a sidevalve Continental 6 placed transversely in the rear of the cab, mated to a Warner three speed manual transmission. The overall length of the cab was 198.5 inches and the wheelbase was 100 inches. Upon completion of the test, this would serve Checker plant staff as an errand car. (Joe Fay collection)

The vehicle must be light if it is to operate economically. Keeping weight to a minimum means that the entire vehicle must be as compact as possible without any sacrifice in passenger space.'

The project progressed to the development of a mule. Designated the Model C, it utilized a sidevalve Continental 6 placed transversely in the rear, mated to a Warner three speed manual transmission. The overall length of the cab was 198.5 inches and the wheelbase was 100 inches. As was always the case with Checker being an "assembled car", many components for the Model C were sourced from the "parts bin" of other makers and independent component producers. In the case of the test mule, the front and rear suspension, brakes and wheels were from Studebaker.

The test mule went through extensive testing, and the results were poor. Shortly before his death, Snow recounted to automotive writer Karl Ludvigsen the facts behind the project's end:

'The objections to this design were that a vehicle of this type with the engine mounted in the rear behind the rear axle cannot have good weight distribution on a short wheelbase. There was too much weight on the rear wheels for good roadability and performance. Furthermore we had passenger seats facing each other as in trains and this we considered would be very objectionable to the passengers who rode backwards in the front seat.'

With poor handling and questionable passenger comfort, the project was killed.

In the summer of 1945, Snow moved on to a new project, the Checker Model D. Like the Model C, it too was equally unconventional. It would be a front wheel drive vehicle with a transverse engine mounted forward of the front axle. Plans called for a significant number of variations to be produced, including sedans, limos, station wagons, coupes, convertibles and light trucks. Having designed the Cord 810 front drive system, Snow would bring an extensive amount of experience to the table. Dietrich would handle the exterior design.

An artist's rendition of the Model D. Proposed as a front wheel drive vehicle with a transverse engine, mounted forward of the cab, plans called for a significant number of variations to be produced, including sedans, limos, station wagons, coupes, convertibles and light trucks. This artist rendition depicts a "woody" sedan. (Joe Fay collection)

Two running prototypes, a five-passenger sedan and a seven-passenger taxicab were developed. The prototypes were equipped with a transverse mounted Continental 6-cylinder engine mated to a 3-speed manual transmission. The prototypes rode on a 112-inch wheelbase within a total length of 189.5 inches, six inches shorter than the 1946 Ford sedan and a foot shorter than the Model C prototype. The Dietrich styling was quite attractive and current. Unlike the Model A, its front end styling was well integrated into the overall design of the car, bearing a very close resemblance to the 1941 Chrysler. The end result was that the compact little cars were effective, efficient and stunning to boot.

The two prototypes were tested for well over 100,000 miles. The taxicab was tested in real taxi service, accumulating over 35,000 miles and the sedan ran in tests totalling over 65,000 miles. According to Snow, quoted in *Special Interest Autos* Magazine in 1973:

'The passengers commented on the excellent ride qualities and the drivers claimed it was easy to keep on the road, handled well in traffic and on the highway.'

Tested in the early winter, according to Snow:

'In heavy blizzards under adverse road conditions, it performed exceptionally well, pulling out from curbs blocked with snow without difficulty.'

Although both vehicles tested well, in the end it appeared that the Model D would have a higher cost per unit to produce. Tests also indicated that maintenance cost for the more complex FWD Checker would be higher than taxi operators would find acceptable. The Model D project was killed in 1946, which left Checker with a major problem. The company had not produced a car in close to five years and whatever Markin had done with the body tooling, there was none left from the Model A to continue production in the post war years.

In addition to the major issue of not having a new car ready to produce and sell, Checker

The project Model D moved to a very advanced state of design. Dietrich built two wood bucks, including this, for the five-passenger pleasure car. Note the second, taxi buck at an earlier stage of construction, just visible in the right background. (Joe Fay collection)

The taxicab was tested in real taxi service, accumulating over 35,000 miles in Racine, Wisconsin. According to designer Herb Snow, passenger and driver feedback was extremely positive. (Joe Fay collection)

The Model D project killed, Checker rapidly developed the Model A2. The body passenger compartment of the A2 is virtually identical to the Model D, the only difference being the length of the front clip, which was redesigned to accept the front-mounted Continental 6-cylinder flathead engine and rear wheel drive configuration of the Model A. The Checker A2 dimensions were consistent with most large US produced automobiles at a total length of 205.5 inches and the wheelbase 124 inches. (Joe Fay collection)

also had an another problem that needed to be addressed quickly. Checker owned thousands of cabs in a number of major US cities, including Chicago, New York, Pittsburgh and Minneapolis. The current fleet was operating vehicles that had long outlived their useful life as cabs and needed to be replaced immediately.

Checker rapidly developed a replacement for the Model A, combining the chassis and engine configuration of the original Model A with the Dietrich designed body of the Model D. The resulting vehicle was called the Model A2. The body passenger compartment of the A2 is virtually identical to the Model D, the only difference being the length of the front clip, which was redesign to be configured for a front in line Continental 6-cylinder flathead engine and rear wheel drive configuration of the Model A. The Checker A2 dimensions were consistent with

most large US produced automobiles at a total length of 205.5 inches and a wheelbase of 124 inches.

The Model A2 was developed in less than one year and was introduced to the public on December 15 1946 in *Automotive Industries* Magazine. It was a stylish car with pontoon fenders that flowed into the doors, a classic long hood and curvaceous passenger cabin. The body line behind the windshield was comparable with the styling on other classic cars of the period. Missing from the Model A were the driver roof vent, the glass roof and the landaulet opening roof. The introduction of the ground-breaking post war automotive designs by Studebaker and Ford would make Checkers look old again.

The following year, in August of 1947 Checker introduced another model, the A3. Called a pleasure car, this automobile was

The A4. New features for the A4 and A5 included new, lower rocker panels for improved driver entry, larger windshield and side windows for improved visibility and wraparound bumpers. There was also a new hood ornament and gravel shields for the rear fenders. (Joe Fay collection)

Checker's first official entry into the non-taxi market, a car that could be sold into the "Black Car" limo markets that were growing in most US cities. A deluxe version of the A2, the A3 sported a bench front seat and more chrome. The Checker A3 was equipped with a rear trunk. This was the first time Checker had offered a trunk as standard equipment. The A2 did not have a trunk, mainly because many US cities still had laws on the books that prohibited taxis equipped with trunks. Many of these laws dated back to the prohibition era as rum-runners would transport illegal booze out of sight of the police in the trunks of taxicabs.

A re-engineered Checker was introduced in 1950. This was the Model A4, with its companion, the Model A5 pleasure car. Both models featured a tighter turning radius and wraparound bumpers that bore a striking resemblance to the 1940s era Cadillac bumpers. The

A4 and A5 also sported new rocker panels for improved driver entry and larger side windows for improved passenger visibility. Both vehicles were equipped with a fully functioning trunk. The A4 also had a unique feature: an electrically operated opening rear window, which improved ventilation for rear passengers.

In 1953 Checker again re-engineered the Model A to produce the Model A6 taxi and Model A7 pleasure car. The most significant change was in the passenger area, where the entire roof was raised to improve rear headroom clearance, squaring up its appearance. Other changes to the Model A6 taxi included the introduction of fibreglass, plastic and vinyl and linoleum floors in the passenger compartment. These changes allowed taxi operators to hose down the interiors nightly for hygiene purposes.

The taxicab industry in the US has always been a tough one to engage in, and more importantly

Above: *the Model A5 pleasure car. This Model A5 would have been used in the private car limo trade in New York or Chicago.*

Below: *Checker offered an electronic rear window opening option on the A4 and A5. Similar to an option available on Packard taxicabs, the system was designed by Trico company and provided the taxicab driver with push button control of the rear window. The feature provided passengers with an open air experience similar to the Checker landaulets of the 1920s and 1930s.*

Above: two new Checkers; a Model A5 (left) and a model A4 being used for promotion in South America. Note the fancy add-on roof rack and sun visor on the A5. (Joe Fay collection)

Below: this proud, unidentified driver stands next to his ride, a Chicago Yellow Cab number 1063 sometime in 1952. In the 1950s Chicago cabbies would typically wear black slacks, collared shirts with a bow tie, a light jacket and hat. (Joe Fay collection)

Above: *Checker's Parmalee Transportation Company utilized a fleet of special bodied A4 wagons, in this case a six-door version. It's unclear whether Checker produced the complete car, or subcontracted to another coachbuilder such as Stageway in Arkansas, a company that did produce eight door limos for Checker in the late 1950s.*

Below: *painted in primer, this Checker Model A2 is in knock down form, probably headed to a special coach builder for a special service purpose. Many were exported outside of the US for funeral car service. No knock-downs are known to exist today.*

The Model A was again re-engineered for 1953 to produce the Model A6 taxi and Model A7 pleasure car. The most significant change was in the rear roof, which was raised to improve rear headroom. This Checker is painted in the standard Checker factory approved paint scheme of yellow and green. Many independent taxicab operators would simply stencil their respective cab company above the Checker shield decal on the rear door. The rate card on the driver doors shows the standard New York City rates. (Joe Fay collection)

operate profitably in. Over the course of the last century, taxicab operators had to deal with organized crime, unions, fluctuating gas prices and government regulations. New York City has always posed challenges; according to the American Taxicab Association 1953 Datebook, New York City ranked 45th in taxi per citizen ratios out of the 50 largest cities in the US. For every one NYC Taxicab Medallion, there was one cab for every 669 citizens, about one half of the average of 1349 riders per taxicab. Essentially there were more cabs in NYC fighting each other in the mean streets for fewer passengers than the majority of other major US cities would allow. Additionally in NYC taxicab rates were regulated and metered, a sixty-dollar annual fee was levied on drivers and all were required to carry the cost of insurance. Driving a cab in NYC was a costly operation.

In New York, the Taxicab Commission required that cabs have a wheelbase greater than 120 inches. The law protected passengers from owner-operators who would potentially reduce costs by using smaller vehicles and thus present the buying public with an inferior ride experience in a cramped cab. In a city that makes a significant amount of money on the tourist trade, a bad taxi experience was in essence a potential blemish on the city's reputation. It may be a nice law for families travelling on vacation, the reality was that all surveys and supporting data indicated that it was very rare for taxis to make trips carrying more than two passengers. The result of these regulations was that 11,796 large, lumbering DeSotos, Packards and Checkers battled each other in hand to hand combat for a small number of passengers and equally small profits.

Faced with rising costs during the post war period, cab drivers and operators in New York lobbied for change. The drivers received significant support from Ford and GM, who would be very happy to enter the Taxicab market in New York. Both auto makers saw an opportunity to sell Fords and Chevys into taxi service; hundreds of sales could be had if the law was changed.

The law was changed for 1954, which presented a major problem for Checker as well as for DeSoto, Packard having left the market several years earlier. The new laws in NYC made Checker and DeSoto taxicabs obsolete and uncompetitive. New York and Chicago were Checker's largest markets, with Checker essentially holding a monopoly on Taxicab medallions in Chicago, although not in New York. By the summer of 1954 Ford, Chevy and Plymouth taxis were on the streets of New York City. In December of 1954, all Checker taxicab production ceased. Could the little cab producer survive?

4
The A8 to the A12E - Checker Motors, 1956 - 1982

The A8 design would allow for a vehicle of 199.5 inches in length that rode on a 120 inch wheelbase. When compared to the its new competitors the Checker Model A8 had better hip room, legroom and headroom for both passengers and driver. Additionally the Checker Model A8 had a shorter turning radius, shorter front and rear overhang and superior "angle of departure", all metrics that are critical to city taxicab driving. (Joe Fay collection)

To do more than survive, Checker would have to introduce a new taxi to the market that could compete. So serious was the problem, in 1955 the company took one year out to develop a new cab. As was the case with the Model A2, Checker would refine and re-engineer the original Model A underpinnings for a new taxicab, but this time, major modifications would be in order. The resulting design would eliminate the front I-beam axle and introduce modern coil

sprung independent front suspension with ball joints. The design would utilize components already available on thousands of parts shelves and bins across the US, such as Thompson Industries suspension parts built to 1955 Ford specifications and Studebaker steering system, brakes and wheels.

Two models were introduced for 1956, the Model A8 Standard and the Model A8 Drivermatic Special. The Special was the higher end

The body was totally new in 1956, the Checker now possessed a sleeker slab-sided styling consistent with most US automobiles designed in the early 50's. In order for Checker to comply with the New York ordinance and still fit eight passengers, Checker had to offer a taller design that allowed for a more upright, chair like seating. (Joe Fay collection)

A product of the parts bin, the Checker front headlight bezels were lifted from the Willys Aero sedan and the parking lights were from the Kaiser Henry J. Overall front end styling was quite pleasant, with subtle styling cues stolen from the 1953 Packard. Vented ports on each side of the grille delivered air into the passenger compartment. (Joe Fay collection)

A new fleet of Checker A8s ready to serve Parsippany & Newark, New Jersey area. (Joe Fay collection)

vehicle and came equipped with power steering, a Borg Warner automatic transmission and power brakes. The Standard was a bare bones taxi with unassisted brakes and steering and manual transmission. Both models were purpose built taxis with interior trimming comparable to the previous Model A6. Both could be ordered with an opening electric rear window.

The body was totally new, with sleeker, slab-sided styling consistent with most US automobiles of the time. US automotive styling of the late 1950s moved toward lower and wider designs, but in order for Checker to comply with the New York wheelbase ordinance and still fit eight passengers, Checker had to buck the styling trend and offer a taller design that allowed for more upright, chair-like seating. Rear jump seats allowed the new Checker Model A8 to seat 8

passengers.

In the end this design would allow for a vehicle of 199.5 inches in length that rode on a 120-inch wheelbase. When compared to the other new entries in the taxicab market, such as Ford, Chevy and Plymouth, the new Checker Model A8 had better hip room, legroom and headroom for both passengers and driver. Again when compared to the competition the Checker Model A8 had a shorter turning radius, shorter front and rear overhang and superior "angle of departure"; all metrics that are critical to city driving. The purpose built design gave taxi buyers an opportunity to buy a better cab that was far more competitive in the taxicab marketplace. So competitive, this ultimate taxicab design would be the benchmark in the taxicab industry for the next twenty-five years.

Above: another new fleet of Checker A8s for the Checker Cab Co (city unknown). All were equipped with two-way radio for rapid dispatch. (Joe Fay collection)

Below: this fleet of new Checker A8s, acquired by Yellow Cab Co is destined to serve Gulfport, Louisiana. Note the Avis Rent-a-Car ads on the front fenders. Both Avis and Hertz corporate identities are rooted in the taxicab industry. (Joe Fay collection)

Above: six shiny new Checker A8's ready to serve the Lynwood, Compton and Southgate, California operated by the South East Taxi Company. (Joe Fay collection)

Below: another new fleet of Checker A8s serving Yellow Cab Co. (Joe Fay collection)

Above and below: fitting with Checker's speciality car manufacturer status, Checker offered various purpose built vehicles. Included in the line of A8s was the Adaptomobile ambulance, otherwise referred to as a Cabulance. The bench seat was replaced by a driver bucket seat, allowing for a stretcher to be place on the right side of the compartment. A year later Checker would offer a similar vehicle, the Medi-Car. (Joe Fay collection)

The heavy duty nature of Checker is displayed with this rather spartan interior, painted in a Hammerite textured silver paint. The floor is a solid piece of linoleum and steel armrests with manufacturer plates in full view create a personal "subway car" environment. Door panels are made of vinyl and fibreglass and the rubber surrounds are moulded in grey rather than the standard automotive black rubber. The interior is waterproof, with the floor sloping towards the doors to allow the taxicab operator to hose it down. (Joe Fay collection)

The Model A8 was the first Checker taxicab to offer a full bench seat, effectively increasing the number of passengers that it could accommodate compared to the previous Model A6. In theory the Model A8 could carry as many as seven paying passengers. (Joe Fay collection)

The front clip of the Checker A8 was entirely bolt-on. Assuming there wasn't any radiator damage, this wrecked new Checker could be back on the street within about four hours! (Ben Merkel collection)

Total passenger seating capacity in the rear was five adults. The two jump seats were canted to the right for easy exit curb side exits. This vehicle appears to be painted in the Checker New York City National Cab colours, a white body with green accents. (Joe Fay collection)

The restyled Checker could be very pretty, as this nearly new A9L shows. The "L" meant that the cab was equipped with the time tested, Continental Red Seal 226ci 95bhp flathead motor, which was the only motor available to them at this time. Checker wasn't the only one still using flathead motors, as Plymouth used one until 1960 and Studebaker up to 1961. The transmissions were either the 2-speed automatic or standard three-speed stick shift on the column, which, for a few dollars extra, Checker would put on the floor. The two-tone paint, Checker Special decals, full wheel covers, and checkerboard along the roof were the most obvious options visible. The New York City taxi rates were normally installed at the factory and this tradition continued until 1982. By this time, when an A9 was ordered with available automatic transmission, power steering, power brakes, power driver's seat and even air conditioning, it made driving a Checker in a busy place like Manhattan or Chicago much more pleasant when compared to just a few years earlier. (Henry Winningham)

In the April 1958 issue of *Motor Trend* magazine, a road test of the Checker Model A8 was followed by speculation about the rumoured upcoming attempt by Checker to compete with the major car makers in the civilian car market. *Motor Trend* even went to Kalamazoo and interviewed Morris Markin about the mystery car, but didn't learn much except that the new body dies were being prepared and everybody would be "surprised" when the updated design came out. *Motor Trend* speculated that, to compete in the big leagues, Checker would have to up the horsepower, upgrade the interiors and add more chrome to the exteriors in an era when chrome sold cars. Besides sketching up a fairly inaccurate rendering of what the new Checker model might look like, *Motor Trend* opined

that the new car, unlike virtually all the other lower priced brands sold in the late 1950s would probably have an automatic transmission with power steering and brakes as standard equipment. Their educated guesses were interesting but only moderately accurate.

When the big change finally landed in October, it came in the form of a mildly restyled Checker with the utterly fashionable four headlights instead of two. What made this so remarkable was that, in 1957, the use of four headlights was so new that several Detroit manufacturers got in hot water by building some models with four headlights and selling them in states where the feature wasn't yet legal. So when Checker came out with the much-anticipated Model A9, the four eyes were the first thing people

Here it is! The common-sense car America asked for

Superba 4-door sedan

THE *Superba* BY CHECKER

brings comfort back
to motoring

The A10 Superba line, the new name for the equivalent model to the predecessor pleasure car was finally announced in late 1959 and displayed only trim differences between it and the working A9 taxi model. The entry level sedan offering was called the Superba Standard which, at a starting price of $2,542.42 was nearly devoid of exterior trim and came with the 226ci Continental Red Seal flathead motor and three speed manual transmission on the column. In this artist's rendering of a Superba Standard, it is depicted with the $24.07 option of a two-tone paint job, which came in no less than six possible colour combinations. Customers had four different tyre sizes to choose from and each of them cost from a low of $28.55 for 6.70x15 6-ply blackwalls to $42.30 for the 7.10x15 6-ply blackwalls. Whitewall tyres cost an extra $15.96 for any size. The Superba Standard interiors were very utilitarian, with basic seats and rubber mat flooring that, at least in the rear, could be upgraded to carpet for only $7.08. Round jump seats were extra, too, at $31.53 for the vinyl covering and $42.47 for the nylon cloth.

No matter which Checker model you chose, there was a specific owner's manual waiting for you in the glove box.

For only $107.60, Checker buyers could upgrade to the A10 Superba Special, which was basically a trimmed up version of the Standard with chrome spears along the sides, Superba nameplates, nylon cloth upholstery and carpeting in the rear. It also came with the standard 95bhp flathead six, but the newly offered 125bhp overhead valve version of the Continental Red Seal 226ci six was only $56.63 more. The transmission options were limited, depending on which motor you ordered: the flathead motor only came with a choice of a three speed manual or two speed automatic for $222.28. With the OHV engine you could have a dual range automatic costing $247.76 or a three speed manual with overdrive for $107.60. An under-the-dash Eaton air conditioning unit could be ordered for a pricey $410.68, although few were bought. This particular Superba Special is pictured in the Checker showroom with optional two-tone paint, full wheel covers, whitewall tyres and music radio, all added for $70.22. By May 1961 the Superba Special had become the Checker Marathon, probably in an effort to end the public's confusion over the two Superba models.

noticed. What they didn't notice, since the car had roughly the same body shape, was that from bumper to bumper, virtually every piece of sheet metal was different, including the roof. *Motor Trend* continued to follow the Checker story and, in May 1959, reported that Checker intended to introduce the civilian version of the A9 taxi at the New York Imported Car Show in April. Speculation had been rife about the civilian car project for so long that Motor Trend indicated they would only believe this launching date when they saw private Checkers running around the streets.

The Model A9 turned out to be the last major restyling that Checker ever did, although it is doubtful that the stylists could have imagined that their facelift would last nearly a quarter

century. Checker sales were being helped by Detroit's insistence on low slung sedans, which were not only hard to get in and out of, but many were completely restyled every 12 months. This meant that taxicab operators had to stock body spares for specific years. Checker used to poke fun at Detroit's skimpy interiors with advertising slogans such as "End tiny taxi squeeze", or "Oh, my aching back", and "That's funny, you don't look like a contortionist". Detroit wasn't unduly worried about tiny Checker Motors and refused to fight for the miniscule taxi market beyond tweaking their police car packages to suit commercial interests. To put it in perspective, out of 135,000 taxis operating in the US around this time, approximately 35,000 were Checkers.

The rear seating area of the Superba Special wasn't very cab like, with carpeting and nylon cloth upholstery on the rear seat and jump seats. By early 1961, you could get the rear seat moved forward nearly 10 inches for additional trunk space at a modest $31.53 although this left no room for the jump seats. At this time, Checker wasn't yet building cars with suspended vinyl headliners, so they used the same type of cardboard found in their A9 taxis. For those desiring a taste of luxury, the 1961 A10 Marathon buyer could turn their ride into a mini-limousine with a $212.37 full broadcloth interior, a $63.71 front power seat and a nifty $27.60 chrome rear foot rest that folded forward when not in use. Power windows were not yet available, but they would be soon. Neither Cadillac, Lincoln nor Imperial panicked at the news that Checker was trying to lure some customers away.

The dashboard of either Superba was a pleasing and functional design, which won praise from many a road tester who had become jaded with Detroit's love affair for warning lights instead of gauges. Science and Mechanics magazine called the Checker gauge cluster "lovely". This plastic three-spoke steering wheel would only be used for one year, replaced in 1961 by a four-spoke design that, with a few internal changes, would be used until 1969. The basic dash itself was the same as the A9 taxi and would last, with minor alterations, until the end of production in 1982.

Checker - the All-American Taxi

The ultra-big news from Checker was the new $2,896.37 Superba Standard station wagon which, when compared to the gigantic station wagons that Detroit was putting out in 1960, packed a lot of space into a modest size. It wasn't just a taxi with a rear roof tacked on, because the whole roof, rear inner fenders and rear sheet metal was unique to the wagon. The rear bumper had a dip in it for the license plate, whereas the sedan used the same straight bumper front and rear. This attractive 1960 A10W Superba Special Station Wagon was parked on a street in Kalamazoo; the optional full wheel covers and whitewall tyres really suburbanised it well. Prices for the A10W Superba Special wagon began at $3,003.97, but a $134.29 roof rack and two-tone paint for $24.07 could have dolled it up even further. The tailgate glass was operated by a hand crank, but you could have the power option for $35.39, as fitted on this car. The power tailgates had a sliding lid over a keyhole where the manual crank would normally be. The Superba Standard A10W station wagon had a plainer interior and no side trim. All wagon models came with the OHV 6 cylinder engine only.

There was ample room for three adults in the back seat of the 1960 Checker A10 Superba Special Station Wagon, but the position of the folding seat didn't allow space for jump seats. Carpeting came as standard equipment in the Special. The cardboard headliner was used in wagons and Aerobuses for their entire run, since it came in sections which could be easily removed to service the wiring in the ceiling, just like in the A9 taxis. The Standard model had patterned vinyl seats without any nylon cloth inserts. The rear door bodies were the same as the sedan, but the rear door glass and removable window frames were different.

In an automotive coup, Checker showed Detroit how things were done in Kalamazoo when it introduced a motorized rear seat in its new wagon. The woman in this Superba Special wagon is doing something that would normally be a chore, but flicking a switch on the dash is the only action she needs to take. For $70.79, Checker would install a power rear seat, possibly to go with the $63.71 power front seat and the $35.39 electric tailgate glass for those who cherished the hum of a labour saving device. On the 1962 and 1963 wagons, Checker made you buy the 80-amp battery for an extra $12.03 if you wanted the power rear seat. Perhaps owners were demonstrating this unique feature to amazed friends so much that it was running down the batteries! This wagon is loaded with two tone paint, roof rack, music radio, whitewalls and big hubcaps. Air conditioning was a rare option on Checkers in those days and it wasn't installed on this car. Surprisingly, the power rear seat wasn't very popular and was dropped from the option list for 1964.

Checker was also aggressively pursuing the European market with some rectangular jump seats that were attached to the same mounting as the single, round jump seat. Why they weren't promoted in the US is up for conjecture, but Sweden, Denmark and Switzerland were just three of the big importers of Checkers during the 1960s. The legs on the side were to handle heavy loads. Since Checker made their own seat cushions, they would regularly make the rear seat cushion shorter to help with this export setup.

Checker - the All-American Taxi

After years of having its products stretched by outside body manufacturers like Armbruster-Stageway of Fort Smith, Arkansas, Checker introduced its own line of six and eight door wagons for sale beginning in March, 1961 under the "Aerobus" nameplate. All were built from scratch and had their own braking system, heavy-duty wheel rims, 7.00x15 commercial tyres and special rear axle. Shown is the rare, $5,005.43 six door A10WS6 Aerobus, which like its larger, $5,430.72 eight door sibling, came with the same 226ci OHV Continental Red Seal six that was found in the regular four door wagons. Transmissions were limited to a three speed manual shift or, on the six door only, a heavy duty, two-speed Warner automatic box was used, not the dual range unit introduced the year before. The eight door models had such tepid acceleration that, when equipped with the $850.12 dual air conditioning system, a kickdown switch cut off the cool air when the gas pedal was floored. Unlike the four door wagons meant for the public, Aerobuses came with fixed rear seats unless fold-down ones were specially ordered. Even the rear inner fenders were designed for a fixed seat and conversion to a folding seat later was not possible. This was done, most likely, to allow the cargo area to be stuffed with baggage without impacting the people in the last seat.

To protect the cargo area glass from being broken by aggressive baggage loading, this bus has the optional $31.15 steel grilles along the rear quarter windows, tailgate glass, and a combination Plexiglass and steel grille ($28.32) between the last seat and the cargo area to prevent the stacked bags from coming forward in a panic stop. A mostly wooden roof rack cost $126.80 without a tarpaulin cover or $199.25 with. By special order, a customer could get a long, wooden roof box with lockable compartments for storing things that shouldn't get wet, like band instruments or athletics equipment. To prevent a power tailgate window from burning out due to constant, commercial use, Checker offered the option of two tailgate motors instead of one for $60.73, or almost double the cost for the single motor setup.

The early 1962 A10 Checker front end dated back to the 1958 A9 and featured a star grille with the turn signals inset. The bumper guards were standard.

For Checker, the 1962 models were their 40th anniversary products, and to celebrate, the exterior and interior of their cars was mildly restyled. The first big change came in the front end styling, where the previous star grille was replaced with a full width mesh design and the turn signals were moved to locations under the headlights. The straight front bumper had given way to the dipped design found previously on the station wagon rear ends and Checker raised it a few inches to make the car look a little less boxy. On either design, the far ends of the grille were air intakes with flexible hoses that carried the air to the firewall and into the interior of the vehicle. A Consumer Reports magazine test of a 1969 Marathon felt that these air intakes could bring in exhaust fumes from the car ahead, but in reality, if you're sniffing the burnt hydrocarbons of the vehicle in front of you, the chances are good that you are trying to stuff your Checker up their exhaust pipe.

Checker - the All-American Taxi

In January 1962, somebody at Checker has convinced one of their secretaries to step into the frozen backyard and on to the snow that covers Michigan every winter, to pose next to the A12 Marathon prototype. This year, the A9 taxi model graduated to the Model A11 while the civilian A10 Superbas, Marathons and Aerobuses became A12s. Aside from the updated front end, the new civilian dashboard was designed to further separate the private car from the taxi. Prices for the A12 began at $2,641.50 for the Superba sedan and the Marathon cost $2,793 with companion station wagons at about $300 more. Marathons came in eight standard colours whereas the A11 taxis came in any paint job the buyer desired. The rows of A9 taxis in the background are worthy of attention, as these older model Checkers are nearly extinct today.

The new 1962 A12 dashboard was quite attractive and functional, although it was not the easiest to work on. The padded top did not come off and there wasn't an access panel at that time, so to fix something you had to go up underneath. The black and white gauges had been replaced with more colourful dials with orange pointers and green numerals. The glove box was handily located in the middle and it dropped down so you wouldn't lose your trinkets when looking for a map. The four-spoke steering wheel, introduced the year before, was pretty but the pot metal A12 horn ring was not tough and broke easily. If this car had the $382.26 optional air conditioning, the cool air would have come out of round outlets at each edge of the dash and a rectangular outlet at the front of the transmission hump. All of the A12 models, including the Aerobus used the new dashboard.

The $2,641.50 Superba sedan was now the entry level 1962 civilian Checker. Its upscale brethren, the Superba Special, had morphed into the Marathon in 1961. Sporting very little exterior chrome, this car came standard with the Continental flathead 6 cylinder and three speed manual, but our subject car has the optional OHV Continental six and overdrive transmission, which cost $56.63 and $107.60 respectively. The only outward change to the 1962 models were that the slightly bobbed rear fenders from the eight door Aerobus were extended to the rest of the line so that it was a little easier to replace rear tyres. This A10 Superba also has the $14.21 full wheel covers, two tone paint $24.07, and $75.04 AM tube radio. (Joe Pollard)

The A11 taxi dash was basically a warmed over version of the 1956 A8 dashboard and it still didn't have a stitch of padding. The four-spoke steering wheel had the cute, standard horn button instead of the flimsy A12 horn ring, which was a good thing for cabbies since they sometimes will use the horn a lot in heavy traffic. This A11 has the optional three speed manual transmission mounted on the floor, which was a measly $18.40 extra over the standard column shifter, which became problematic with age. Checker continued to use Warner Gear automatic and manual transmissions, even after the switch to Chevrolet power in 1964. The dimmer switch has been moved up to below the ignition on this cab because the floor position would get wet, causing switch failure and that usually resulted in the flickering or complete loss of headlights.

The standard rear seating area of the A12E model with optional, large jump seats was typically done up in tough vinyl and this particular car displayed the optional, $27.60 chrome foot rail.

If you had an itch for luxury back in 1963, you could get that itch scratched at Checker by ordering the broadcloth interior, as shown in this Custom Limousine. From the power windows, priced at $104.77 to the $162.82 sliding partition, this interior didn't resemble the A11 taxi model much, even though they were kissing cousins from different sides of the tracks. The rear air conditioning controls and music radio were built into the area above where the rear seat armrest folded up. Window switches were down by the ashtrays and the chrome footrest was there to provide a bit more comfort for the coddled passengers.

While the switch to Chevrolet power in February 1964 was pretty big news, Checker wasn't done yet and introduced a taxi version of the A12E Custom Limousine called, appropriately enough the A11E. Priced at $2,963.63, it came with a 230ci Chevrolet six and three-speed manual on the column. The rectangular jump seats were $127.42 and the full wheel covers looked nice for only $14.21. The "Checker" script on the front wings and boot lid were optional. This car was dubbed the "supercab" because it could hold up to nine people and was designed for tours, hotels and general municipal uses. Few cab operators ordered the long wheelbase taxis, because for most of them, the large passenger capacity was overkill; most rides only involve one or two people.

The rear compartment of the A11E was done up for commercial use with rubber flooring, vinyl seats, and an aluminium scuff plate to protect the bottom of the door panels. It was a far cry from the Custom Limousine interior but, underneath their varied exteriors, they were the same car.

Checker - the All-American Taxi

The $2092.45 1965 A11 taxi model hadn't changed too much over the years and it was still devoid of side chrome and trim around the front and back glasses. in February 1964 Checker put Chevrolet's 230ci six into the taxi, which was generally welcomed. Now cab companies could buy engine parts from their local Chevrolet dealer instead of seeking out a Continental Red Seal outlet. Parts for the Continental flathead motors weren't hard to find, but the OHV six wasn't common and finding parts for it was a chore. The OHV wasn't a bad motor, but it lacked the easy serviceability of the flathead and developed a reputation for cracking its expensive head when it overheated. The dashboard of the A11 had changed very little since 1962 but the Checker winged emblem on the boot lid was dropped from all lines in mid 1964, which was a pity.

While Aerobuses used the Chrysler V8 motor (see lower caption, page 62), Checker put the Chevrolet 230ci six and optional 283ci Chevrolet V8s into their sedan and wagon line up. By the following January, the 327ci Chevrolet V8 was an option list for the A12 and, as of April 1965, became the only power plant offered in Aerobuses. On A12 sedans like this 1965 with the 283ci V8, a "V8" emblem, borrowed from the Studebaker parts bin came after the Marathon script on the sides only. A11 models with optional V8s and Aerobuses generally didn't wear this emblem. A basic A12 like this one was priced from $2,813.50, with $110.43 extra for the V8 motor; dual range automatic, $247.76; power steering, $76; power brakes, $42; radio, $75.04; full wheel covers $14.21 and whitewall tyres, $31.75. Checker products equipped this way were very pleasant cars to drive. The A12 Superba line was dropped after the 1964 model year and all the civilian cars became A12 Marathons. For those wanting a plain sedan, they could buy an A11 taxi model.

In the mid 1960s, Checker introduced a bulletproof partition for its taxi models, which was nothing like the sliding window privacy divider found in the Custom Limousine. The cab driver had an electric switch that controlled the smaller, thick glass while the larger piece was fixed. Normally, these partition units were accompanied by a bucket seat for the driver and Checker recommended the $104.77 power windows as well, for a first line of defence against a possible bad person. The bulletproof glass was produced by the Pittsburgh Plate Glass Company.

Here is how the window looked when partially retracted. There was a single arm, electric, window regulator hidden under an upholstered, metal cover. According to tests by a research lab, these heavy partitions could stop both .45 calibre and .357 metal-piercing bullets. Since they required a lot of wiring to install, these shields were not generally transferable to a new Checker and usually got junked when the host cab was recycled. These old style partitions, used until the early 1970s, are extremely rare today.

Above: *for being such a small company, Checker did things that the Big Three car makers would not do, such as installing an English-made diesel motor into their 1969 car line. Checker added the suffix "D" to the ends of certain A12 serial numbers to denote the diesel power plant option. The 80bhp 4-cylinder Perkins 4.236 was mated to the dual range Borg Warner automatic after experimentation that had been going on since 1966. This oil-burner project was supposedly born from a request by Israel for large, diesel sedans that could be put into jitney service. Since the Perkins was available in all A12 Checker Marathon models, some US cab operators tried a few out and generally liked them. On the plus side were 30mpg in overall driving and they would start in 10 degrees below freezing. The negatives were a 60mph top speed and the loud diesel drone. The Diesel Conversion Package included power steering, power brakes and heavy-duty shock absorbers. Oddities included a gear driven accessory drive off of the timing case. Checker advertised their new diesel offerings as being "at least $500 less than the only other comparably equipped diesel car", referring to, most likely the Mercedes Benz 200D automatic. Unfortunately, the push for an economical, large sedan fell on deaf ears and Checker quit promoting the conversion in the US, although they continued to build them for export as late as 1975. Many of the Perkins powered cars were A12ED Marathon sedans with jump seats, as shown by this very pretty late 1968 edition. For 1968, Checker made the front and rear glasses taller, added some test tube wood grain to the A12 dashboard, replaced the 283ci V8 with a 307ci V8, upgraded the brakes to a dual system and began installing the same basic hubcaps that Studebaker used to use.*

Right: *from February 1963 to April 1965, Checker installed the Chrysler 326ci V8 into both the six- and eight-door Aerobuses in an effort to improve their anaemic performance. The V8 gave sixty-five more horses and was coupled to a three-speed manual transmission. These buses were called the models A12W6C and A12W8C, the C meaning they had Chrysler power. This happened around the same time that Checker experimented with some Plymouth 225ci slant-six motors in taxis. The Chrysler V8s were not shared with the Superba or Marathon lines. Also around this time, Checker lengthened the front door skins a little and got rid of the small spacer between the front and rear doors.*

Upjohn Corporation, a pharmaceuticals company located in Checker's hometown of Kalamazoo was a regular buyer of eight-door Aerobuses until at least the early 1970s and here is one of their fleet from the 1963 era, Number 31. Noticeable options on this bus were the roof clearance lights, music radio and rear baggage cage. Upjohn also purchased a white A11 much later in 1981 for use as a factory security car.

Above: 1969 was the end of one low production model run at Checker and the start of another. The handy little six door A12W6M Aerobus was killed off on October 1 after only 26 were built in that year. The numbers had been going down from highs of 37 in 1966 and 39 in 1967, down to only 18 in 1968. To put that in perspective, Checker sold 278 eight-door Aerobuses in 1968 and 436 in 1969. The final six-door cars were all powered by the ubiquitous Chevrolet 327ci V8, putting out 185bhp through a three-speed, column change manual transmission. The dual range Borg-Warner automatic could be specified as well as a nifty four-speed stick on the floor, which hardly anybody ordered. Since 1965, the Aerobus models had special rear outer fenders with large wheel cut-outs, because changing a rear flat on an older bus with the sedan-type fender skirt was tough unless the tyre was skinny. The Aerobuses still had their own unique brakes, rear axle, wheel rims, and centre doors when compared to a standard, assembly line A12W Marathon wagon. By this time, government safety regulations had begun to take hold and the 1969 A12W6M six door Aerobus, being basically a nine passenger wagon found itself in a grey area in terms of safety requirements. Considering the miniscule sales numbers, it wasn't worth it for Checker to make the six-door conform to the same standards that recently designed Detroit station wagons had to meet. Conversely, because the eight-door Aerobuses could hold twelve passengers they were classified as commercial vehicles and therefore exempt from car standards. For example, no Aerobuses came with headrests or shoulder belts, and seat belts for passengers were optional all the way to the last buses in 1977. This 1968 six-door has optional clearance lights on the roof, a $31.44 extra

Above: the A12W Marathon station wagon was a handy car with over 92 cubic feet of cargo space, but it was a hauler that only a few wanted to take home and put to work. The "Little Giant", as Checker called it, began the 1974 model year with a retail price of $4,972.65. It was still listed in July but was gone by autumn, with only 23 built. Its standard equipment pretty much mirrored the Marathon sedan, except for wagon-only items like the $85.50 chrome roof rack. The full wheel covers and whitewall tyres were extra, at $14.87 and $30 respectively, but the $109.07 Chevrolet 350ci V8 was not available in California. A two tone paint job was still available on any Marathon for only $22.37, which helped to break up the boxy lines a little.

Above, left: while the six-door Aerobus was dying a thousand deaths in one part of the Checker factory, an unusual variation of an existing product was taking shape in another building. Where the idea came from for this new model is currently unknown, but it was an idea ten years ahead if its time. For many years, wheelchair users were forced to ride in stock sedans, because vans of that time period were crude, rode poorly and Detroit didn't have a stock vehicle that wouldn't require expensive coachwork to be wheelchair accessible. Checker saw a new niche forming and, after years of catering to special needs buyers, created a high top sedan specifically designed for medical patient transport. They called it the Medicar. While ambulance makers frequently used a fibreglass cap to add several feet to the roofs of their creations, Checker actually took three pieces of sheet steel, formed them, and welded the pieces together to make the domed top. While most were A12E Marathons with vinyl roofs, a handful were A11Es without the vinyl top or Marathon dashboard. In 1970, the second year of production, the price of a Medicar began at $5,682.54 and came standard with the 250ci Chevrolet straight-six motor, Borg-Warner dual range automatic, power front disc brakes, one bucket seat for the driver and 180-degree rear door hinges. Unique options included a $48.50 wheelchair ramp that could be stored in the trunk, an additional removable bucket passenger seat at $117.79, and a removable, rectangular jump seat cost $86.61. Air conditioning was $346.45 and the upgrade to the now available 350ci Chevrolet V8 which, at only $114.87 didn't break the bank. Not many were sold, however: 1970 came in at 26, and in 1971, its final year, only 18 were constructed. Employees at the factory referred to this car as the "Guppy", which was the nickname for a high-topped transport plane of the same time period.

Left: the late comedienne Phyllis Diller had this 1972 Checker A12W Marathon station wagon from new and was nice enough to autograph pictures for author Ben Merkel and the Checker parts vendor, Joe Pollard. For Ms Diller, the Checker was a going-to-the-airport car as opposed to the other ride in her Beverly Hills driveway, a Rolls Royce. Ordered in all polar white, the $4,113.18 wagon came with the 250ci Chevrolet six and dual range Borg-Warner automatic, since the stick shift transmission had been discontinued in 1969. Major options on Ms Diller's wagon were a chrome roof rack at $85.50, front air conditioning for $361.84 and power steering, costing $70.63. Power steering was a required and needed option on V8 equipped cars. Minor extras included the full hubcaps for a paltry $15.66, whitewall tyres, and $11.75 for two front bumper guards as the station wagon models weren't available with rear guards due to the tailgate. The cost of the A12W Marathon wagon to the Checker dealer was $2,877.00. As per new federal lighting regulations, Checker had to enlarge the front turn signals, add lighted side markers and increase the taillight area, which it did by making all four rear lights red and moving the back up lights to the rear valance.

Above, left: the 1973 Checker was a car in transition. New federal bumper standards were requiring that cars had to be able to withstand a 5mph collision without damage. Considering the size of the new aluminium bumpers, the joke amongst Checker collectors is that the factory thought that the Feds said a 50mph hit instead of 5! To satisfy the law, two energy absorbing shocks were mounted behind the front, chrome bumper that made it stick out a few more inches than it used to and the subtle difference can be seen on this 1973 A11 that belonged to the Fort Cab Company of Waynesville, Missouri. The rear bumper was not yet subjected to the 5mph rule but that was only temporary. To those used to the chrome bumpers, the new look took some getting used to. This was also the last year for a standard, chrome grille and tail light bezels on the A11 as these items were now painted a semi-dull silver instead. The dual range Borg-Warner automatic transmission finally got replaced with a GM Turbo 400 long tail automatic that was considered by many to be an improvement. Starting prices for the 1973 began rolling at $3,850, with the longer A11E coming in around $500 more.

Left: as this 1974 A12 Marathon displays, the ends of the new Federal bumpers came with plastic extensions, which were fragile and easily broken. This initial bumper set-up only lasted a year before being upgraded to an all-aluminium affair without plastic ends. In an awkward attempt to hide the bumper shocks and brackets, the factory used a crude piece of vinyl that used to flop around when the wind caught it. In practical, Checker tradition, the front and rear bumpers were interchangeable. All the 1973 models except the Aerobuses got the government issue fat lip. In hindsight, while Checker's execution of the bumper regulations was perhaps a bit heavy handed, a look at some other car manufacturer's responses to these same regulations absolves 2016 N Pitcher Street of any guilt.

Above: while the 260 Aerobuses assembled in 1973 escaped the aluminium bumper treatment, the last 154 1974 wagon-based editions finally got the whoppers, as evidenced by the back half of this Long Island Airports Limousine. Note also the new taillights and lighted side markers, changed in accordance with federal laws and mentioned in the caption to the picture at the bottom of page 64. A new 1974 Aerobus with dual air conditioning, roof rack, and a few minor extras could set you back $6,655.27 with the standard 350ci V8 and GM Turbo 400 automatic. Unfortunately, the death of the A12W station wagon also signalled the swan song for the A12W8 Aerobus, since they shared the same body tooling. The final station wagon buses were built in November 1974 and they would not be back. Issues for the Aerobus stemmed from the fact that van-based minibuses had improved a lot and were encroaching deeply into former eight-door station wagon territory. The demise of the station wagon body left just the Marathon and A11 four door sedans to soldier on in regular or long wheelbase form.

Checker - the All-American Taxi

Above, left: *the last production line A12 Marathon built, serial number 1CMMS4524CK001920, is this comely 1982 example, ordered by the late Gilbert Ellington of Hendersonville, North Carolina, who specified a 229ci Chevrolet V6, air conditioning and the saddle tan vinyl interior. His car was built at such a late date, July 7 1982 that he had to order the factory propane option to get a new Marathon at all. Such a car priced out at $10,950 with an additional $750 for front air conditioning and $275 to secure the LPG fuel package. Only 88 of these A12s were built this year and 21 of them ran on propane. The production numbers for its fancier sibling, the $12,025 Marathon A12E long wheelbase sedan were even an more diminutive 17. At the time of writing, this historic white Checker was being used as a food tour car in New York City.*

Left: *like Lazarus rising from the grave, persistent requests for the Aerobus kept trickling into Checker during 1975 so, in 1976 a prototype eight-door sedan was constructed using the A12E nine passenger four door as a base. The end result is pictured here behind the factory in the 1990s wearing fancy, chromed headlight bezels and full vinyl top. With four full bench seats and two, rectangular jumps, the new bus could handle fifteen passengers and was called, appropriately, the Aerobus 15 or Model A128E. In basic form, it cost $9,460 with the Chevrolet 350ci V8, automatic transmission, power steering and brakes, two under seat heaters, five 9.50x16.5 truck tyres, West Coast type commercial mirrors, tinted glass, lap belt for the driver and full hubcaps set into Ford truck trim rings. Unlike the station wagon Aerobuses that used drum brakes all round, the new models had a heavy duty front disc brake set up with eight-lug truck rims. The only real issue with these long sedans was that trunk room wasn't anywhere near capable of carrying fifteen people's luggage, especially if the $1,120 dual air conditioning was ordered, since the rear A/C unit hogged some of the already precious baggage space. The only solution was to spring for the $395 wooden roof rack with complimentary tarpaulin, but in reality it was almost impossible to keep passenger's stuff totally dry in downpour conditions. A lot of custom work went into these creations and some of it can be seen in the special cut-out front outer fenders that now matched the cut-out rears. The front floorboards and rear inner fenders were modified to keep the truck tyres from scraping, and since Checker made their own seats, the rear cushions were made narrower to accommodate the changes. The commercial turn signals, of which there were two in front and two in back, ran out at $66. Because Aerobuses were exempt from car safety requirements, there were no headrests and a buyer had to pay $40 for each shoulder belt and $12 for each passenger's lap belt. Underneath, even though the Marathons and taxis had to have catalytic converters from 1976, the Aerobuses did not have to have one. A mere 60 were built in 1976 and only 47 in 1977, their final year.*

Above: *for those desiring a nine-passenger sedan in 1979, the pickings were very slim: Checker or Cadillac. Changes to the Marathon and taxi line were mostly confined to the engine choices which, as of 1976 included the Chevrolet 305ci V8 in addition to the standard 250ci 6 and 350ci V8. Since the equipment that had to be fitted to comply with smog regulations had caused a drop in horsepower for every GM motor, Checker made the 305ci V8 standard in all E models beginning in 1975. A 350ci Oldsmobile diesel V8 was offered from late 1978 until 1981, after GM's Ed Cole pushed for it once he began working at Checker. Following the Chevrolet Impala's lead, the 250ci 6 was replaced by a 229ci V6 later in 1979 in an effort to improve fuel economy. The front-end suspension got a final makeover in mid-1979, which would be the last big change that Checker would ever do. This rare and imposing 1979 A11E Community Cab was spotted at Chicago's O'Hare Airport in 1984 and had not only a few battle scars from traffic but sported two different cab numbers on its left front fender. Prices for Checkers this year began at around $7,000 for the standard A11 taxi model and went to almost $10,000 for a Marathon A12E long wheelbase sedan.*

5
The Checker Factory

The early nineteen-twenties were a tough time for auto manufacturers and Kalamazoo, Michigan. Being a burgeoning automotive hub, the city wound up with some empty factories and the accompanying loss of tax revenue when the Handley-Knight and Dort car companies went belly-up. The city fathers were most pleased when Checker moved from Joliet, Illinois in May 1923 because, unlike the failed brands before them, Checker had proven itself a viable and growing business concern which could absorb some of Kalamazoo's unemployed. What made it more of a coup was the fact that, back in March, Checker had nearly purchased the Mitchell Motors plant in Racine, Wisconsin. The switch to Kalamazoo sent the Mitchell Motors property into receivership.

Initially, the 80 x 800-feet Handley-Knight plant, built in 1920 was used for final assembly after the bodies had been constructed across town at the 200,000 sq ft, four storey Dort facility, which Checker also purchased. The whole transaction was said to have involved between $2m and $3m, a tidy sum in those days. Until the Dort property was ready to produce cab bodies, Checker contracted with body companies in Springfield, Massachusetts and Indianapolis, Indiana to supply them with cab bodies in the meantime.

In 1924, there wtre nearly 400 workers building about 20 cabs per day, which was still a normal day's production almost 60 years later. While the assembly line had been up-to-date in 1920, it didn't change much over the decades, and by 1982 had become a rather quaint anachronism of a bygone era when cars were built by hand and records were kept in ledgers, not computers. By 1930, Checker had constructed a new Plant Two to add on to Plant One, the Handley-Knight facility at 2016 North Pitcher Street. Here they consolidated the cab making operation at the one location and then disposed of the Dort building, the original Plant Two.

After the taxi production line went down in 1982, Checker focused on making parts for, primarily General Motors. In 1988, for example, Checker was making tailgates for the Dodge Dakota, Chevrolet Suburban, Blazer and S-10 Blazer, in addition to van doors and cowls. In 2009, it had been making parts for the Buick Lacrosse and Cadillac CTS.

On June 9, 2009, Checker entered bankruptcy proceedings, closed the plant and the new owners moved the production lines elsewhere. Most of its physical assets were sold for $950,000 while the remaining contracts for General Motors went for $650,000. By November, most of the factory had been stripped of valuables and was razed to save on property taxes. The remaining building, which had contained the executive offices was vandalized and burned the following year. Today, there is very little left to mark the spot where nearly a quarter of a million interesting cars were built. At least Morris Markin's nearby house remains and is now a public park, called, appropriately, Markin Glen Park.

This aerial photo of the Checker factory, taken around 1956 gives a good view of the 38-acre site, with North Pitcher Street going vertically along the left. The main entrance and offices are in the lower left corner with the sales building at around the ten o'clock position north of the main office. The right side of the property is bordered by a railroad track with convenient sidings into the plant, where Checker kept their diesel locomotive. In the field behind the factory, long rows of new cabs can be seen along with what is probably a day's output sitting at the rear of the long, Plant One building on the left. The decorative oval with the pointed shrub in front of the main offices was removed by the 1970s and a circular test track was constructed, about this time, where the new cars are lined up in the back. The plant itself was designed by Mills, Rhines, Bellman and Nordoff of Toledo, Ohio using lots of glass to let in natural light. These panes of glass did let in a lot of light, but unfortunately they also allowed plenty of heat to escape, so Checker sprayed insulating foam over many of them during the 1970s in an effort to control energy costs.

Whilst for practicality's sake the mechanicals and electrical fittings of Checker cars were bought elsewhere, the sheet metal and interiors were Checker-only parts that the company cranked out for themselves. Shown is a worker removing a single roof stamping from one of the gigantic presses that Checker employed. Because of the large amount of hand labour used in assembling its cars, no two Checkers are exactly alike and some parts that should be identical might be slightly different when you try to interchange them, because of who might have made those parts that day. To cite a few examples of homespun variations, the checkerboard stripes along the sides of a cab weren't always in the same place on cars of the same year and the hole for the optional rear door locks that was manually drilled into the far left on each dashboard was rarely in the same place on each cab ordered with it. Sometimes, the switch itself was crooked. To make stubborn doors fit an opening, workers regularly used wooden two-by-fours to nurse the truculent portals into place. While this may sound crude today, it must be remembered that Checker was, first and foremost, a hand built, low production commercial vehicle that only cost about 20% more than a mass-produced Chevrolet or Ford taxi. The company's loyal customers were into money-making functionality and generally not consumed by aesthetic details such as uneven body gaps or slight orange peel in a paint job.

Checker A4 bodyshells move down the assembly line in Kalamazoo. Except that the shapes of the cars would be different, this scene would remain essentially the same for another thirty years (Joe Fay collection)

The pet locomotive that Checker kept inside the plant for moving railroad cars around. To make sure that Number One diesel wasn't mistaken for anybody else's equipment, they marked it clearly for all to see. (Erich Lachmann)

Above: *the Checker Motors' main office building looked like this in February 1982, and sported a fine row of its own products. Those staff members in a higher position were regularly rewarded with company cars that were frequently loaded with options like air conditioning and vinyl roofs with opera windows. Many times, these models were sold and replaced unless the possessor bought the car outright from the factory, which some did after the assembly line quit in 1982. Checker routinely overhauled some of these cars during the 1990s if the owner was in good standing with management.*

Above, right: *the top parking spots to the right of the Checker entrance were taken by a stately pair of late model long wheelbase Marathon A12E sedans. Presumably they must have been for the use of some company big-wigs. The one on the left is a 1980 model and its sister ship is one of only five 1981 examples built with the 350ci Oldsmobile V8 diesel motor. Two others were ordered by a funeral home in Pocatello, Idaho but one has to wonder whether the racket of the diesel motors was an appropriate sound for the serenity of the cemetery. After service, both of those cars wound up being painted yellow and used as cabs. The base price for a 1980 A12E was a hefty $11,771 but that included a vinyl top and V8 engine as standard equipment. Its companion 1981 diesel began at $12,866 and went up from there with air conditioning at $711 for front and $1,211 for dual. The dual air conditioners had a unit in the trunk that blew cold air out of the rear parcel shelf, although this did take up some of the luggage space. The big rectangular jump seats would set you back another $382. With a liberal use of the option sheet, the price of the cars could be cranked up to $14,000 without too much trouble.*

Right: *This 1981 A11 propane prototype was parked next to its upscale brethren, identified by its special "Propane" roof sign. The licence plate was a Michigan Manufacturer's plate, so it was probably a test mule for the upcoming $222.75 propane option that Checker offered on their A11 and A12 sedans only. Many experimentals had very low serial numbers, often ending with an 001 or 002. Near the end of cab production, buyers were limited to engine choices as nearly all the gasoline V6s had been spoken for by April 1982, leaving the propane V6 and the 270ci Chevrolet gasoline V8 as the only engine choices for last-minute buyers. After production ended in July, a lot of people who initially wanted gasoline cars bought propane models when it became clear that this was their last chance to buy a new Checker from the dealer or factory. There were some persistent rumours that production might start up again but, after the last assembly line car had been completed on July 12 1982, much of the tooling required to build the classic A11 was removed, which made future auto production very unlikely.*

Checker - the All-American Taxi

Above; above, right; below, right: *most of the Checker company cars were more colourful and less formal than what management was driving but they were loaded with options, as displayed by this trio of white-topped 1981 or 1982 regular wheelbase sedans parked in front of the main offices. Whilst two are clearly labelled as Marathons, the third (below, right) probably is too, but not knowing the serial number, it could be a well-optioned A11 dressed up like a Marathon. The 1981 and 1982 models are overtly identifiable from the rear by two licence plate lights instead of the single one used up to 1980. When Checker's Cab Service garage would refurbish one of their own vehicles, they didn't adhere to the strict rules of originality and would use whatever paint or trim they felt like using or what was currently available in the shop. All of these flashy sedans had whitewall tyres and chrome gravel shields and the taillight housings, which normally were painted dull silver were chrome plated. The bumper guards were made by the Gem Guard Company of Chicago and were not offered on the official option list but were a popular dealer-installed accessory, along with the stainless steel vent shades for the windows. Unfortunately, out of all the company cars used at Checker Motors, only one is known to exist today.*

Checker - the All-American Taxi

Above: the assistant to the president of Checker Motors, Rod Walton still had this nice company car at his disposal in 1988 and it is shown here behind the factory's Cab Service building after it had just come out of the shop. It was a mildly customized 1979 long wheelbase sedan, but whether it was an unlabelled Marathon A12E or a dolled-up A11E is currently unknown. The landau vinyl top, oval window, chrome headlight bezels, body coloured bumpers and B-post opera lights point to it being a possible product of Florida's Southeast Checker Sales in Fort Lauderdale, but Checker Motors could also have done all of those touches in their own Cab Service garage. The lack of a hood ornament or any chrome script wasn't that unusual, as Checker regularly deleted it on formal cars to tone down an upscale model's direct kinship to the working taxis at the airport.

Above, right: being a car manufacturer, it was normal for Checker to keep a couple of cars around for general, all-purpose use like making parts runs to town or picking up a customer at the bus station. A typical Checker Motors "gopher" car was this blue pre-1978 jumbo E model with its Checker logo on the front doors. While it was probably an A12E Marathon, the chrome script was left off so its true identity could be questioned today. What is clear, though, is that the car had been overhauled at some point in the Checker workshops, because the windshield wipers met in the middle, which meant a pre-1978 car, but the angled gas filler is the type introduced on the 1978 models, so this part had been replaced with a newer panel, probably due to corrosion. The vinyl skirt below this panel is also of the later, 1980 to 1982 type where Checker crudely stapled it to try and hide the guts of the energy absorbing bumpers.

Right: This 1982 A12 Marathon was living proof that you could order a new Checker with whatever paint job you wished, and if it wasn't one of the 200 choices in the Checker paint pattern book, then you could sketch one up yourself. This car used the diagonal design of paint pattern 205, which was used by a few cab companies but rare on a private Marathon. Even the bumpers were painted to match the lower body. This car was ordered as a factory demonstrator, with many options including vinyl top, opera windows, air conditioning, 270ci Chevrolet V8, Trac-Loc rear axle and black velour interior with jump seats.

Checker - the All-American Taxi

Above: aside from interesting paint patterns, choosing pink on a boxy car like this 1981 Checker A11 was an easy way to get noticed by nearly everybody. Our subject car was parked at the factory in February, 1982 with Illinois dealer plates but it could have been one of three 1981 A11s ordered by Central Management Corporation of Phoenix, Arizona, with front air conditioning, grey interior and round jump seats. The boot lid has the optional "T" handle lock instead of the usual key lock and is accompanied by an optional chrome grab handle, mounted a few inches above it. This grab handle was useful in preventing drivers from using and breaking off the relatively fragile T handle when slamming the boot closed. No 1982 Checkers were ordered in pink.

Above, right: In February 1982, some brand new Checkers were waiting patiently for their new owners to come for them. The pretty Marathon A12 on the right was a pleasant butterscotch colour and, while it had the chrome gravel shields, no $290 vinyl top or opera window ($342) were ordered. The Firestone 721 white sidewall tyres ran $87 and were a popular Marathon option, but cab companies rarely ordered whitewalls, not only because of their extra expense but they were easily scuffed up and mismatched whitewalls can make any cab look a little junky. The base price of the Marathon A12 in 1982 was $10,950 and that of the white A11 on the left rang in at $10,360. For about $600, the Marathon owner got a chrome grille, carpet, patterned seats, a suspended vinyl headliner, glue-on side trim and some chrome script that said "Checker Marathon" on the boot lid and "Marathon" on the front wings. After traditional yellow, white was one of the most popular colours on a Checker A11 because they could be used for anything from private transportation to, with the addition of a few decals, a car for hire. Both of these cars were gasoline powered, probably by the 229ci Chevrolet V6.

Right: posing in the Checker Motor Sales showroom is the last assembly line Checker built, serial number 1CMTS4129CK002000, the final edition of 2,000 cars assembled. The order for this last unit was placed on January 11, 1982 as Checker Motor Sales floor stock. It may have been ordered by personally by David Markin, son of Morris Markin, because whoever ordered this cab made sure it wound up being the last one built nearly seven months later, a feat that required a very high amount of corporate authority. The green and ivory exterior, paint pattern 141, looked like a Chicago Checker but there were many differences that set it apart. Whilst all the Chicago Checkers had the Rear Seat Forward option, this last cab had the standard seat set-up in grey vinyl with round jump seats. The second major deviation was that the final Checker runs with a 229ci Chevrolet gasoline V6, whereas all the 1982 Chicago Checkers were straight propane with the same engine. This last production line Checker is currently in the Gilmore Car Museum in Hickory Corners, Michigan and has been driven less than ten miles its entire life.

Above, left: *June 1982 found a colourful assortment of fresh Checkers that would be leaving the factory soon. By this time there were only a few weeks left before production was to halt. The parts had been ordered to complete just 2,000 cars, so late comers had to either buy an existing car or rub a magic lamp and ask to be transported back to late April, 1982, before the factory stopped taking orders. After production ceased on July 12, the phone rang and rang with potential customers who either didn't know that the car had died or they hadn't taken the shutdown notices seriously and were now in a state of panic, but it was too late. Steve Wilson, the Head of Purchasing for Checker, once remarked that, in hindsight, he thought the factory could have sold at least another thousand cars had they been available.*

Left: *Some of the last Checkers produced bided their time in a lot behind the factory in early 1982. Soon, they would be in service and their initial fares would be treated to some of the final whiffs of a freshly-minted Checker cab before several thousand riders made the new cab smell disappear. As can be plainly seen, the preconception that all Checker cabs were yellow is erroneous.*

Above: *a A further pan of the back yard at Checker reveals the sheer volume of cars waiting to be completed. At first glance the line-up, with cars of very similar colours might suggest that both pictures were shot on the same day.*

Even though production of the final edition had been planned for 2,000 cars exactly, when it came time to actually build the units, there weren't enough parts, primarily upholstery material, so Checker was forced to park at least a hundred brand new, almost-finished cars in their oval test track for a few months until the supplies were available. At that time, all the cars were run through the assembly line again and finished off for final delivery. Some customers got tired of waiting and cancelled their orders, but most were anxious to get their last new Checkers even if they were late and a little rusty from sitting in the tall grass for months. Some of the last cabs had mismatched interiors with gray door panels and black seats just to get them done and out the door. To help unload remaining inventory, Checker repainted some existing cars to suit the needs of their waiting customers and routinely discounted the sticker prices by ten percent and more without the customer even asking for it. (Byron Babbish)

6
Buying a Checker

There were three ways to buy a Checker car, beginning with the factory and their Checker Motors Sales dealership, right up the road at 2142 North Pitcher Street. Here, you could order a car and, after a few worrying weeks, enjoy the rare treat of going to pick up your new vehicle right at the factory, which many buyers did. Normally, this kind of experience is reserved for high-end cars, but Checker did it every day with taxis, Marathons, and Aerobuses. The showroom was not modern and could only handle a couple of automobiles, but for the Checker loyal it was akin to visiting a maternity room and shrine combined. There were no high-pressure salesmen, no five-year payment plans and no huge pushes to move the old cars out, because the new cars looked like the old ones. The buying process was simplicity in itself: you chose your options, gave a deposit and waited until Checker notified you of the car's completion. If you had the itch to buy a Checker right then and there, a couple of new cars were for sale at all times or,

if a buyer developed heart-shaped eyes for one of the company cars, the executive driving that car would normally relinquish the keys so that it could be sold. The upside for the displaced exec was that a new Checker would be coming soon to replace it.

A second possibility for purchasing a new Checker was from an authorized dealer. There were of about 45 in 1972, a number which was virtually halved by 1980. Although Checkers were always available to civilians before 1958, the factory push for the private market began around then and picked up steam in 1960. Before the official Checker dealers came along, you could get parts and cars from many of the 26 nationwide parts outlets that were also operating cab companies. The reason for the dealer effort was probably to make up the loss of sales due to changing taxi market conditions. For example, since New York City had allowed ordinary family sedans to be used as taxis since 1954, the DeSoto Skyviews and Checkers were no longer

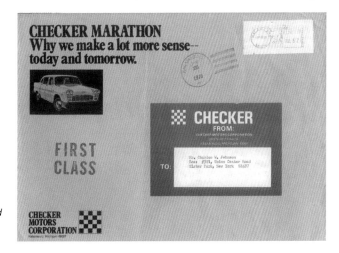

For years, Checker used envelopes like this to send brochures and information to interested buyers. This one was sent in 1976.

The Checker Motors Sales Corporation building at 2142 North Pitcher Street not only housed the showroom, but also had a Cab Service Corporation sited behind it for repairs. Shown here in 1965, the showroom had new cars, ordered as floor stock, for anybody who wanted to come in and buy one immediately. While the details of the transaction shown are currently unknown, it can be presumed that the two gentlemen on the right are purchasing a vehicle from the salesman on the left, probably the Aerobus and maybe the long wheelbase Marathon A12E directly behind them. The two men on the right could also be part of a dealer drive-a-way, where the cars were to be driven to a dealership as floor stock or delivered to waiting customers. It wasn't unusual for tow bars to be used on drive-a-ways to move more than one Checker at one time, especially with taxis.

required by law and many fleets switched to those cheaper, mass-produced sedans, mostly at Checker's expense, because DeSoto buyers could opt for a Plymouth or Dodge and stay under Chrysler's wing. In the bigger picture, Checker no longer owned as many fleets as it used to, so its time-tested formula of selling a lot of cabs to themselves wasn't working as well as it had in past years.

It does appear that the dealer push was effective, since by 1963 about 40 per cent of production constituted private cars, although this number went down to around 20 per cent in 1972 and ended up at less than 10 per cent by 1982. Interestingly, Checker's founder, Morris Markin didn't drive his own products, stating once in *Time Magazine*, "I don't know exactly why, but I've always had General Motors cars."

Of the dealers outside of the factory, five were attached to subsidiaries of Checker Motors Corporation, known as Cab Service and Parts Corporation outlets. As the name implies, these were factory authorized Checker parts depots and service garages with locations at the factory, Long Island City, New York, Brookline, Massachusetts, Alhambra, California, and Chicago, Illinois. Most of the dealers, however, were small and attached to other, larger, automobile endeavours. To lure existing dealers to take on the Checker brand as a sideline, the factory issued cheeky brochures asking if the dealership owner wanted to become a member of the "I like $500 bills" club, referring to the possible profit from the sale of each car. There was even a badge with that logo to be worn at sales meetings. Some dealers, like Denver's Colorado Checker Sales

1992, and the Checker Motors Sales building hadn't changed much since 1965. The garage door had been upgraded to a roll-up and the glass windows on the right were made much smaller, probably to save heating costs. The sign had been changed from Checker Motors Sales Corporation to Checker Motors, Sales/Service/Parts and the telephone poles removed but, other than those obvious differences, things were pretty much the same as they always had been! Inside the showroom, Checker kept a few special new cars for public display, but none were for sale unless you knew the right people and had some cash. The building is shown during a Checker Club of America get-together at the factory in June, 1992 and the gold 1972 Marathon A12W station wagon parked in front belonged to the late Checker club president, Steve Wilson and the black and red 1960 Superba A10W standard wagon to its immediate left belongs to Don McHenry, the founder and first president of the Checker Club. Inside the building, visitors could gawk at the racks of new parts, which were not for sale. The Cab Service garage was still functioning in the early 21st century, but by this time most of the Checkers still in the shop were restoration projects for the Markin family. (Jay Hinkhouse)

and the Bahamas' Freeport Taxi Company were also bases for large cab operations that used, not surprisingly, nearly all Checkers.

The third way to get your hands on a new Checker was to order the vehicle by mail. From the initial inquiry, Checker would send out some sales literature with an option list, price sheet, and colour chart. Once this was filled in and returned to Checker Motors, a purchase agreement would be sent to the customer requiring a $500 deposit. Normally, the build process took a few weeks, sometimes longer. When the new unit was constructed, the choice was to either take delivery at the factory or have the new unit shipped by truck. Many buyers made an event out of going to Kalamazoo so they could not only save on shipping charges but also indulge themselves in the factory-direct sales experience. If a purchaser took a plane, bus, or train to Kalamazoo, the factory would normally send one of their marked blue sedans to pick up the expectant owner. Once delivery of the gleaming new Checker was accomplished, the sales department would also assist with either getting a Michigan temporary plate, or they were known to allow customers to borrow a Checker Sales dealer plate for the trip home on the understanding that it would be sent back upon arrival.

Checker - the All-American Taxi

Above: in what must have been 1965's dealer drive-a-way of the year, the late David Markin (Morris's son) waves and smiles from a golf cart, justifiably proud of the amazing line-up of cars. Remarkably, this included only one taxi, in the back row! For independent car manufacturers, drive-a-ways were a good, time-tested way to get dealers revved up for a couple of days before they all drove their new Checkers home. At typical drive-a-way events, awards were given out, speeches made and dealers got a chance to develop a personal relationship with not only each other but the support staff at the factory.

Above, right: many of the cars in this picture have large Checker banners in their rear windows, presumably to advertise the product on the way home. It must have been an impressive sight to see dozens of brand new Checkers together on the highway!

Right: it was normal for car dealers to experiment with a product display at a county fair and Turnpike Super Service, Inc in Middletown, New York tried it around 1964 at the local Orange County Fair, presenting a single Marathon. While attracting a lot of curious people, no attendees impulsively pulled the sales trigger, so the fair display wasn't repeated the following year. Checker had all sorts of sales banners and propaganda materials for the motivated dealer. (Erich Lachmann)

Checker - the All-American Taxi

Above: the largest dealer outside of Kalamazoo was most likely Marvin Winkoff's Checker Motors Sales Corporation in Long Island City, New York, one of the Cab Service and Parts Corporation outlets mentioned on page 86. Strategically located right across the river from Manhattan, the 35-30 38th Street dealership looked like this in 1980. Since it was an official outlet, this was the place to buy parts or get your Checker serviced, because there were many specialized parts on a Checker that you could not buy from your local auto parts store. The back lot, visible here, was packed with brand new Checkers, mostly ordered as "floor stock", which meant that they were available for anybody who walked in the door. Checker Motors Sales moved to this site in 1972 from 419 East 60th Street in New York City, probably because real estate was cheaper in Long Island City than Manhattan. A yellow 1976 A11 belonging to the Minute Men Cab Company was parked outside with a note under the left wiper blade. It had the rare and expensive $651.32 roof-mounted air conditioning condenser, which cost nearly twice as much as a regular A/C unit. These were good for keeping things cooler in very hot conditions, but if one of the high pressure lines that ran up the right centre post sprang a leak, the explosive release of freon into the cab interior was a fairly shocking event for drivers and passengers alike.

Above, right: this pair of 1980 A11E jumbos are sitting pretty at Checker Motors Sales, waiting for their owner to come for them. They were ordered by the Long Island Airports Limousine Service, or LIALS for short, a company that ran a large fleet of blue Checker A11Es out of Hauppauge, New York until the late 1980s. Every day these familiar Checkers would run from the suburbs of Long Island to Kennedy and LaGuardia airports and back, using two-way radios to coordinate passenger pick ups. The beginning retail price for these husky sedans began at $8,782, about $2,000 more than the dealer paid for it. To this was added front air-conditioning at $579, large jump seats at $329 and glued on side mouldings for $48.50. Before leaving the lot, the dealership would add hubcaps and its signature strap iron bumper guards to protect the front and rear sheet metal in heavy traffic. The final outfitting, including the addition of a large roof rack, two way radios and company lettering, was done at the LIALS garage.

Right: the ability to order a new automobile in any colour was a fun option for Checker buyers. A case in point is this light green Marathon A12E that was probably an ordered unit as it is doubtful that a sales department would order a large, relatively expensive sedan like this one in a colour that made it look like a dish of lime sherbet. With a price beginning at $9,653, it came standard with the vinyl top and 270ci Chevrolet V8. Air conditioning, large jump seats, and 307ci Chevrolet V8 were extra cost options. A 350ci Oldsmobile V8 diesel was also available for this car, but with only seven built, it is unlikely that this is one of those. The lack of "Diesel" script on the left side of the trunk lid also suggests gasoline power.

Checker - the All-American Taxi

Above: Checker Motors Sales' dealer plates on this 1979 Marathon A12 indicate that this is a demonstrator and, as such, it was heavily optioned with a formal vinyl top, chrome gravel shields, white wall tyres, rubber bumper guards and window vent shades. To get this top configuration it was first necessary to order the elimination of the rear triangular windows, known as Code #188, for $131.50 before you could install the vinyl top, which was another $230. There was a colour choice with the tops, but, at the factory, customers were pretty much limited to Code 34 black and Code 37 white. To get oval opera windows put into the blanked-out quarter window panels, you had to reach into your billfold for another $263 in addition to the other two previous requirements. Behind this comely Marathon is the entrance to the Cab Service and Parts garage.

Above, right: a couple of taxis were lined up at the entrance to the Cab Service and Parts garage while they awaited their turn for a bay in the Checker taxi hospital. The blue car was a well-used 1970 to 1972 A11 that probably began life as a yellow cab and then, when a few years old was purchased by a livery operator and painted this classic livery blue, which was a commonly used colour at that time to denote a for-hire car, no matter what the brand. Cabs like this tended to have "Livery" licence plates and no taxi roof domes, rate stickers, or even meters. The term "gypsy" cab has been attached to these types of taxis because they weren't as heavily regulated as the yellow, medallion cabs. Odd details include the interesting boot latch used to replace the missing factory latch, and the Aerobus outside mirrors, which were commonly installed on New York City Checkers by Checker Motors Sales to help with driver vision. It is a credit that this car was so old and still making money in the tri-state's punishing environment.

Right: it was entirely possible to purchase an A11 model, which was your basic taxicab and option it up so it almost looked like a Marathon. In 1980, the price difference between an A11 and a Marathon A12 was about $500 and that amount could just about pay for air conditioning. The differences between the two models were in trim only. The Marathon came with a chrome grille, "Checker Marathon" script, rear carpeting, patterned seats, and suspended vinyl headliner. Some buyers didn't like the suspended vinyl headliners because they had a nasty habit of dropping onto passengers' heads when the windows were down on the freeway. The cardboard headliner of the A11 didn't have that problem. This brown 1980 A11, with chrome gravel shields, rubber bumper guards, side trim, optional "Checker" script and window vent shades could almost pass for a Marathon, but it was really just a taxi in disguise.

Checker - the All-American Taxi

Above: a peek inside the Cab Service and Parts garage revealed the variety of Checkers that came here to have work done by mechanics that looked at them every day and knew what parts fit what year of cab, without having to look at a parts book. Since nearly all of the customers brought in working cars, it was critical to get these vehicles on the road again as fast as possible, since time down was money lost.

Below: In 1996, a beat up 1982 ex-NYC Yellow, ex-gypsy, ex-TV cab stopped at 35-30 38th Street, Long Island City, New York, the place where it had been first sold, but found nothing familiar except a few oil stains in the street. Checker Motors Sales Corporation's building had taken on a decidedly medieval look, complete with stain glass windows depicting unicorns. Unfortunately, there was not a single sign present to indicate the use of the structure at that time. As of 2015, the entire site has been replaced with the UA Kaufman Cinema complex. (Ken Smith)

Marvin Winkoff also opened up Checker Southeast Corporation, a combination Saab-Checker dealership in the mid-1970s at 5810 North Federal Highway in Fort Lauderdale, Florida. Later, after the Checker car had died, it turned into Saab of Fort Lauderdale, and this photo shows how it looked in 1986 with the Checker sign still up. Like the New York outlet, this dealer also ordered A11 and A11E models in lots of different colours so they could be customized by local shops in a myriad of ways. From special paint schemes, padded halo tops and fluffy interiors, these dressed-up taxis could be found rubbing elbows with the much more expensive cars at posh country clubs and nightspots in the Miami area and all around the country. By the late 1980s, however, most well heeled owners had stepped out of their now-aging custom Checkers and into newer cars. After building several hundred creations each year, a paltry 22 A11s and 3 A11Es were worked over in 1982. The A11 was normally chosen for customising, because the price difference between the Marathon and the taxi model helped pay for some of the special touches. Today, 5810 North Federal Highway is a Dairy Queen restaurant.

While the lavishly decorated Checker Southeast creations, known as "Winkoffs" in the Checker collector world are a matter of personal taste, there is no denying that these flashy cars made a big impression wherever they went, and still do so today. From the chromed headlight and tail light bezels, chrome edging along the body, two-tone paint jobs, B-post opera lights, landau tops, window vent shades, oval windows and wire wheel hubcaps, many customs resembled Wurlitzer juke boxes on wheels, but that's how a lot of Florida folks liked them. In a town like Miami, where Rolls-Royces and Ferraris are common, cruising in a customized Checker was a way to a get noticed without spending an inordinate amount of money. This striking two-tone blue combination, photographed in 1986, began life as a pale blue 1981 A11 taxi. Almost all "Winkoffs" were ordered with front air conditioning.

Above: those without the desire to drive a really flashy car could opt for a more discreet custom like this 1982 A11, which is missing a headlight bezel. Compared to its stablemates, this A11 had the opera lights, velour interior and wire wheel hubcaps, but the exterior was kept quite modest, with a single exterior colour, painted headlight bezels and no vinyl top. A 273ci Chevrolet V8 was under the bonnet.

Below: a brand new 1980 A11 taxi-in-a-tuxedo sits at Southeast Checker in 1981, showing yet another possible theme for the large canvas that is the Checker A11. The blackwall tyres, lack of opera lights and it conservative colour give this car a pin-striped suit appearance. The wire wheel hubcaps, used on many Ft Lauderdale customs, were not very convincing when compared to real McCoy wire wheels. The window sticker to the right of the main Checker one was an Environmental Protection Agency (EPA) sticker, stating that the buyer could expect about 17mpg overall. Checker Southeast had a small additional sticker charge for the trimmings added to the once-plain sedans. (Paul Belanger)

Above: *it was not unusual to see Bahamian taxis in a service bay at Southeast Checker, because getting cars refurbished on the island wasn't the easiest thing to do, and Ft Lauderdale, Florida is a day's ferry ride away from Freeport, Grand Bahama. This 1979 Bahamian A11E appeared to be receiving major mechanical work, since its hood is off. With the Checker Motors factory out of the car game, Southeast Checker was one of the few places left in 1986 that knew how to work on a real car. In 1980, there had been as many as three Checker dealers for the whole state of Florida and oddly, all of them were near Miami.*

Below: *another late 1970s Bahamian A11E peeked out of a service bay as it was being prepped for paint in 1986. With the grille off, it was evident that this cab was originally white and been repainted black and silver in the traditional two-tone treatment favoured by Southeast Checker. The real wire wheels and thick whitewalls definitely made the cab stand out and it must have been quite the island ride when the new paint job was done.*

Checker - the All-American Taxi

Above: while it might have been yellow, this customized 1980 A11 was certainly no taxicab! With real wire wheels and everything else lemony, it presented a regal appearance without being as baroque as some of its stablemates. For being a six-year-old car, this pretty Checker was holding up well, since the salt air of the Florida coast normally wreaks havoc on all cars living near the ocean. For some owners, the Checker custom was a fashion accessory and not their only car, so they were kept garaged when not in use.

Above, right: outside of the major cities, most Checker dealerships were a sideline to a larger business like a major brand car dealer or, as shown here, a motorhome sales outlet. Lipe Motors of Decatur, Illinois had been a Checker dealer since at least 1972 and was actively ordering inventory until the cars quit coming. The lot owner, Harold Lipe ordered these two 1982 Marathon A12 sedans on May 17 and held on to them for a while. Both cars were so close to the end of production that they shared the 229ci Chevrolet V6 with propane fuel, a less popular option with the general public than with cabbies. Most propane Marathons were converted to run on gasoline within a few years after they were purchased. Both cars began at $10,950, with front air conditioning at $750, propane option at $275, Trac-Loc rear, $122, tilt steering wheel, $127, power door locks, $211, AM/FM radio, $237, rear seat speaker, $55, 215x15 whitewall tyres, $87 and chrome fender shields $79 as the major options chosen by Mr Lipe. The green car, built June 17 had tan velour upholstery while the white car, assembled two days earlier, had a saddle (i. e. tan) vinyl interior. Neither car sported round jump seats.

Right: the late Harold Lipe is shown posing with a 1972 Checker Marathon A12E in the fall of 1982. He began Lipe Motors in 1948, moved the business to Decatur in 1966 and retired in 1985. His motto, as seen on all of the stickers placed on the boot lids of his cars for sale: Lipe Motors, a lot of the best!

A lone Checker sits outside of another long time Checker dealer, Turnpike Super Service, Inc in Middletown, New York. Shown here around 1990, Turnpike was started in 1959 by the late Mickey Lachmann with his father as a used car lot and repair garage on busy Route 17. The Checker franchise was acquired around 1962 and continued until Checker quit production in July 1982. Turnpike Service honoured the 12 month, 12,000 mile warranties until July 1983 but serviced Checkers for years after that. Turnpike Service sold up to about 20 cars per year but, interestingly, didn't sell one Aerobus. To save on full freight charges from Kalamazoo, Turnpike would have some of their orders shipped alongside the high volume of taxis going to Checker Motors Sales in Long Island City, a 90 minute drive from Middletown. Two A11 models were regularly kept as floor stock for local cab companies to buy if one of their taxis got totalled: a robin's egg blue one for Syndicate Taxi in Middletown and a red unit tagged for another cab company nearby Port Jervis. Remarkably, one of the Syndicate cabs is still present and was never put into service. Today, Turnpike Super Service Inc is still family owned and continues to sell used cars under the slogan: Home of Fine Automobiles. (Erich Lachmann)

7
The Galva Projects

The Galva II was not Checker's first attempt at a FWD Taxi. That was the Model D. Herbert Snow, formerly of Auburn-Cord-Duesenberg, was commissioned with designer Raymond H Dietrich, formerly from Le Baron, Chrysler and Lincoln to develop the replacement for the Model A. It was determined that FWD technology could not meet the tough standards of the taxi industry. The project was killed and the resulting design was altered to produce the Model A2. (Joe Fay Collection)

By the 1970s the Checker cab design was several automotive generations old. As the decade started the Checker A11 design had been in production for close to twenty years, with design elements that could be attributed to a 1950 clay design and some chassis components with ancestral linkage to the 1939 Model A. Clearly, it was time for Checker to consider developing a modern taxi that would allow the company to produce cars into the next century. Several projects were executed in the early 1970s in the attempt to develop a new Checker. In 1974, US Steel and prototype builder Autodynamics

of Madison Heights, Michigan proposed a new Checker idea called "Galva", from Galvanised Steel", to Checker Motors Corporation (CMC). The plan was to design a new model using newly developed manufacturing techniques to produce a vehicle with a reduced amount of tooling. Unfortunately, the project never got off the drawing board; Checker management was happy, the company was profitable and would continue to produce the A11 and various other speciality cars.

By the mid-seventies Checker would revisit the idea of producing a new taxi. In March

Checker - the All-American Taxi

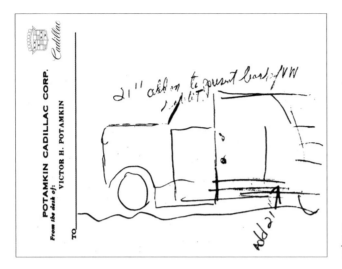

The rough concept drawing of the new Checker from the desk of Victor Potamkin. (Forbes Magazine)

of 1977, Ed Cole, former GM president, and Victor Potamkin, one of the largest car dealers in the US, bought control of Checker Motors' taxi subsidiary, Checker Taxi Co, which then operated Checker fleets in Chicago, Minneapolis and Pittsburgh. Ed Cole was the former general manager of the Chevrolet Motor Division and president of General Motors. In the early 1950s, Cole was the lead engineer in charge of the development of a new Chevy engine built to replace the legendary 'Stovebolt Six' engine. This new engine was Chevrolet's small-block V8, a massive success that remained in produc-

tion into the twenty-first century. Victor Potamkin was a popular New York car salesman who used a combination of sales discounting and aggressive advertising to transform a Manhattan Cadillac agency into the flagship of his $1bn a year automotive empire. At the time, Checker generated net income of $274,000 on $87m in sales. The magic formula of Potamkin's deep financial pockets and sales and marketing know-how, combined with Cole's automotive engineering capabilities and GM connections were the perfect combination required to transform Checker.

Ed Cole and Victor Potamkin partnered with Jim McLernon, President of Volkswagen of America, to explore the feasibility of stretching the VW Rabbit 21.0 inches in order to create a VW based Checker. (Joe Fay Collection)

Autodynamics' publicity photo of the proposed Galva FWD Checker. Although the Rabbit is considered a small car, its quite clear to meet Checker's passenger compartment standards the Galva need to become very large. (Joe Fay Collection)

It was an exciting time - expectations were high that the new partners would revitalize Checker's future, new models would be introduced and the company would grow. Cole and Potamkin partnered with Jim McLernon, President of Volkswagen of America, to explore the feasibility of stretching the VW Rabbit (aka Golf) 21.0 inches (533.4mm) in order to create a VW-based taxicab. The hoopla was significant and the US automotive world was watching Checker when, just weeks into the new partnership, Ed Cole was killed when the private plane he was flying crashed on his way to Kalamazoo.

Despite Cole's death, Checker soldiered on with the transformation plan, and three months after, in August of 1977, they unveiled plans for the new Taxi to the public in a *Forbes Magazine* article. The new Checkers would indeed be based on a Volkswagen Rabbit, stretched by 21 inches (533.4mm) in the rear passenger area and with modifications to the roof in order to improve headroom. To reinforce the overall strength of the Rabbit design, Checker anticipated adding 300lbs (136kg) in weight to the body as structural panels, for a total weight of 2,300lbs (1,043kg). The new taxi would use the same standard Rabbit transmission, but the added weight required new power options. Three power plants were considered; Perkins, Mitsubishi or Oldsmobile diesel engines. The VW based design would have been a serious departure from past Checkers. The passenger compartment would have carried four rear passengers, two facing forward and two facing rearward, one less than the 5-person rear capacity of the current A11. This layout, not found in US taxis may not have met with the approval of passengers, who would have to compete for knee room. Ed Cole's plan assumed sales via GM's dealer network of 50,000 units a year.

After Cole's death, Checker CEO David Markin reduced the sales plan down to 30,000

This artist's rendition of Galva II shows the massive rear doors of the 128-inch wheelbase proposal. (Joe Fay Collection)

This beautiful artist rendition of Galva II could not really hide the fact that the new Checker would essentially be a big box on wheels. (Joe Fay Collection)

units. The bodies would be produced by VW and shipped to Kalamazoo for final assembly. One test mule, a stretched Rabbit was created and field-tested. The test encompassed the placement of 500lb (227kg) of sandbags in the rear passenger area of the vehicle, which was driven from Kalamazoo to Chicago, where it was put into loop traffic and monitored for performance. The resulting test was disappointing. Upon its return to Kalamazoo, the mule was parked and the project was killed as it was decided the VW based concept wasn't suitable as a taxi. For the rest of the decade, Checker would continue to produce the A11.

Galva II design work utilize a Chevy Citation test mule, parked in Kalamazoo, displays an extended rear passenger section. The modern 1970s era design is quite a big change from the 1950s era Checkers parked alongside.

Galva II

By the 1980s, the US had gone through two energy crises, one in 1973 and one in 1979. Clearly it was time for Checker to consider developing a modern fuel-efficient taxi that would allow Checker to produce cars into the next century. In the early 1980s, via a series of financial transactions, David Markin monetised CMC. Potemkin and Cole's widow were paid out and both exited the company. Markin had total control of CMC again and the funds available to produce a new Checker.

Checker's final attempts at introducing a new cab came in early 1981. CMC signed a contract with Autodynamics to develop a new Checker. The project was called Galva II, an extension of the project originally positioned back in 1974. Autodynamics developed a design that would use the latest GM components developed under the GM X-Car program.

The GM X-Car line was a major departure from GM traditional design. It was a front wheel drive platform with a transverse engine, similar to the BMC mini concept. The new Checker was to be front wheel drive; ironic as this concept was first tested by Checker in the mid 1940s with the Model D project. Consistent with the original Galva project, the new Checker would be based on limited tooling. Paul E Newman of Autodynamics was quoted in *Automobile Quarterly*:

"We had a particular build concept for them (Checker). It involved a low cost tooling and break form panels."

Howard E. Klausmeier of Autodynamics was quoted in *Automotive News*;

"The intent is to standardize componentry and simplify tooling and manufacturing as much as possible. The only curved glass will be the windshield. All other glass is flat. In addition, the components provide easy replacement for

Long after the Galva II project was killed, the Citation test mule lies dormant outside the cab services building with various Checker Chicago propane test vehicles. (Ben Merkel Collection)

repair and maintenance using simplified attachment systems."

In November of 1981, Sab Hori, Head of CMC Engineering described more details of the new Checker for automotive writer John Melrose:

"We're going to try and do everything we can to make the cab easy to service. We'll have bolt-on fenders, possibly of plastic, and we're considering bolt-on door panels made from either RIM (reinforced injection moulding) or SMC (sheet moulding compound) plastic because if a panel is damaged it would be easier to replace. The fenders will be friendly, flexible type, like those on Oldsmobile's new sport Omega. We're also thinking about plastic hoods, rear hatch doors and fascias, because the tooling costs are lower. As a low-volume producer, we have the advantage of not worrying about the slow cycle times needed in making plastic parts. And what we're trying to do is go as far as possible with proven technology. Checker is so small that we can't afford to be the leaders; we've got to be followers."

The new Checker would have a fully independent rear suspension. The design was based on a Firestone developed system called the Marsh Mellow. A Marsh Mellow spring is a fabric reinforced rubber cylinder. A striking solution for Checker, the Marsh Mellow spring was known for reliability, corrosion resistance, low cost, and basic simplicity. Best of all from Checker's point of view, unlike a conventional rear leaf spring, if a Marsh Mellow spring fails, the cab would not have been taken off the road immediately. This feature would endear it to taxi fleets. Surely it could handle the pot-holed streets of New York City.

At the time of design, Sab Hori was quoted in *Automotive News*:

"The New Generation of taxicab design will be a four door hatchback designed with identical bumpers, glass, lighting, engines, transmissions, and front/rear-end styling. All four models will have surround-type frames, extended for longer vehicles."

Pulled out of the plant in 2010, the remnants of the Galva II wooden buck was rotting away in a dark section of the CMC plant. Note the Chevy Citation fenders from the test mule were saved along with the buck. (Todd Harroun)

So, like CMC models of the past, several variations of wheelbase and configurations would be available. Plans called for three different wheelbases; 109.0 inches (2,768.6mm) for six passengers, 122.0 inches (3,098.8mm) for eight passengers and 128.0 inches (3,251mm) for seating nine and a raised-roof paratransit vehicle with wheelchair capabilities. David Markin was also quoted in *Automotive News*, stating that the new vehicle would be sold to both fleet operators and private individuals.

There was a lot of excitement, Great press was generated, but ultimately, the new Checker was never put into production. Regarding the decision to kill it, Sab Hori was quoted in *Automobile Quarterly*:

"We were at a crossroads whether to continue to offer the Taxi or discontinue and go into contract work. To stay in the taxi market required a large expenditure of money. At the time, the whole automobile industry was in a downturn. We didn't feel it was worth the expenditure of several million dollars. There was still a lot of uncertainty. It would be a tremendous gamble."

Paul E Newman was also quoted in *Automo-bile Quarterly*. According to Newman:

"We had a lot of engineering completed. There were several variations of clay models and a seating buck. We looked at production engineering. David Markin was relatively young and was quite ambitious for the type of vehicle he was building, but the project died. Partially because it was based on the GM X-car. It had its limitations due to the technology of the time."

As Newman stated, production and engineering were well along. At least one test mule was created based on a stretched Chevy Citation. Clay models were completed, a step typically just ahead of tool and die creation. Design bucks were fabricated. This project moved far beyond the drawing board.

Upon review of the design buck and prototype photos, it's very clear that a new front drive Checker would still be a very big car. The design buck utilized many existing Checker components. The front seat of the buck was actually the same front seat used in the production of the Checker A11, providing over 60 inches of hip room. The buck is not really much smaller than a standard Checker. The overall reduced size was mainly derived from a smaller front clip, utilizing a transverse engine and the elimination of the rear trunk. Based on this framework, it's safe to say that the passenger compartment would have yielded comfort similar to Checker's past production cars. The production 1982 Checker hovered at about 4,000lbs (1,814kg). Assuming that the use of plastics and reduction of vehicle size would have eliminated 800lbs (362.8kg), an educated guess puts the proposed FWD Checker at 3,200lbs (1,451kg). Given the Chevy X-Car weighed approximately 2,300lbs (1,043kg), one has to question whether the new Checker concepts could rely on powertrains designed for vehicles close to 1,000lbs (453.5kg) lighter than the proposed FWD Checker and still produce acceptable performance. Add into the equation larger Checker versions at 122-inch (3,098.8mm) and 128-inch (3,251mm) wheelbase with 8- and 9-passenger capacities, one can only imagine that the X-Car powertrain would be significantly challenged in moving passengers from point A to point B. Given the financial investments required, the state of the economy, the effort required to change production and designs, Checker truly was at the crossroads of their future.

Checker Motors had always run a third party production business that served the US automotive industry. As far back as the 1930s, Checker had produced bodies for Hudson. In the 1950s, they produced trailers for the US Army and Sears Roebuck and during the early post war era supplied the Railway Express Agency with truck bodies used to deliver parcels door to door. During the time that Checker was debating new car production, Checker was producing the Dodge Maxi vans for Chrysler Corporation. Clearly, David Markin had options in terms of making investments either continue to produce automobiles or expand third party production. At the same time that CMC was developing the new Checker, the company was in tough contract discussions with the United Steel Workers. The dynamics at the time made it clear that Checker would not only not produce a new Checker, but ultimately, Checker ended all car production in June of 1982 in order to focus on third party production. Funds to be directed for the new Checker were diverted to a new strategy of third party stamping and production. The expansion kept Checker in business well into the 21st century. Although it's romantic to think about the possibilities of what a new FWD Checker could have achieved, it's safe to say that the decision not to move forward was clearly the correct one.

8
The Last Years of Checker Taxis in Service

A basic, late model Chicago Yellow Checker cruises into Chicago's O'Hare airport, circa 1984. Even though they were the same yellow, Dupont Centari 6554 as New York City's Checkers, they looked different without the stripes. They weren't the same inside, either. While Manhattan taxis had room for five behind the partition with jump seats, Chicago Yellow had the Rear Seat Forward option, which moved the rear seat forward 9 inches to give more luggage space, but took away the space for the jump seats. Few Chicago Checkers had partitions, but all had air conditioning in 1982, whereas New York City was about a 50-50 mix that year. The placement of the front licence plate in the centre of the grille was a Chicago-only item and many Checkers there had it. About 525 Chicago Yellows were assembled in 1982.

The news that Checker Motors had quit making their famous taxicab sent some of their old customers into a quandary, because they had been using Checkers for a long time and that's what they were used to. Customers generally liked them for their generous rear seat room but drivers tended to like them only when they were new and fresh. Many switched to the Chevrolet Impala because they were already familiar with the GM running gear from the Chevy-powered Checkers.

Since many major cites had enacted age restrictions for taxicabs during the 1980s, all Checkers operating in the affected cities were on notice that they would not be growing old in those places. Many fleets trade in their cabs after only two years and those late model taxis go to the suburbs or smaller towns where they are put back to work for as long as is allowed or economical. New York City and Chicago generally allowed about five years maximum to operate so all 1982 vintage taxis were pretty much history by 1988. New York City gave age exemptions to the few remaining Checkers but got in trouble with some owners of clean, other brands who thought that the passes were unfair.

Many of the last Checkers went to places like New York City, Philadelphia, Chicago and Norfolk, Virginia but small numbers of cabs wound up going nearly everywhere, including Alaska, Sweden, Canada and the Bahamas. There was hardly an American city or town that didn't have some Checkers running around in some capacity, so the news that production had ended immediately caused taxi operators to avoid buying used Checkers because they were now orphans.

Unlike New York City, with its all-yellow requirement after 1968, Chicago had no such law, so there were many Checkers with different colour combinations running around. Interestingly, at least two colour combinations were regularly kept in stock at the Checker Motors Sales Corporation dealer at 109 Racine Street: two-tone blue and red and white. The blue combination used a dark blue bottom with a light blue top that could have passed for white. Several taxi companies, like State and Robertson, bought blue cabs and a few independent operators, like Lawrence Rayburn did too. At least six red and white two-tone combinations were available on a Checker and many pretty examples could be seen working for cab companies like Lakeside, Flash, C & D, Willie Hull, Tiger, Choong Soo In, Arigarg and Boone, until the late 1980s.

The Washington DC area wasn't a common place to find Checkers, but a few did wind up there. The hot taxi topic in the nation's capital during the 1980s was the use of a fairly complex zone system form of fare charging instead of utilizing meters, as most cities did. Cabbies had to carry zone maps with pertinent rates to explain the cost of a ride to confused tourists. If you were near a zone border, a walk across the street could have resulted in a cheaper fare. The meter eventually won out in 2007.

Lexington, Kentucky had at least one cab operator using Checker cabs until 1988 and they operated yellow cabs under the Holiday Cab banner and blue Wildcat cabs. Most of the

newer taxis were 1982 factory propane powered units and all of the older taxis, some of them 1979 vintage, had been equipped with a single propane tank in the trunk in addition to the regular gasoline tank. Operators with their own bulk propane tanks could refuel their cabs for less than the cost of gasoline. The big problem for propane cabs is that if you run out of LPG, you're walking unless it's a dual fuel vehicle.

The City of Norfolk, Virginia was one of the Checker hot-spots in the south. Four cab companies in town, Norview Checker, Yellow Cab, Black and White, and East Side Cab all used Checkers until they couldn't buy them anymore. The huge naval base meant that cabs were always moving, and at all hours, to ferry sailors and submariners to either a waiting ship or an inviting watering hole at Virginia Beach. Working air conditioning was required by the city for any cabbie that wanted to pick up at the airport, so virtually all Checker taxis were ordered with air conditioning in this area.

When most people think of yellow Checker cabs, places like New York City and Chicago usually come to mind, not the State of Colorado. Remarkable as it may seem today, there were lots of Checkers in Denver, Aspen, Colorado Springs and Pueblo, to name a few real taxi towns. When travellers flew into Denver up until the late 1980s, they were greeted by a row of Checkers.

If it was 1985 and you flew from Aspen, Colorado to a meeting in Chicago and then on to the Bahamas, you surely could have ridden in Checker taxis all day long! The Bahamas, especially the town of Freeport, was a genuine Checker E model bastion. Not only were nearly all the taxis on the island the rare, jumbo A11E variety but there were lots and lots of them. The Freeport Taxi Company operated the largest Checker fleet on the island and was known for their light blue and red taxis with the white tops. While Freeport ordered mostly new units from Checker, their second-hand cabs were sold, painted another colour, and put back into service by mostly independent operators on the island. Major servicing usually meant shipping the cars back to the Checker dealer in Fort Lauderdale, who was also scouting for privately used, long wheelbase cars to send to the island as cabs. By the mid-1980s, the Bahamian government began to push for more modern taxis by making cab inspections tougher for the old Checkers. Parts became so problematic that Freeport Taxi would buy out cab company's parts inventories on the mainland. As of March, 1988 there were approximately 40 Freeport Taxi Checkers in service but this number dropped to 15 by 1990, and shrank to only 2 by autumn of 1991.

There was a niche market for Checker products in Sweden. A dealer in Uppsala, Kjellberg Invest Ab, bought its last six long wheelbase A11E models in 1981. They weren't much different from their US counterparts except for the deletion of all seat belts and smog equipment. A kilometre speedometer, all amber side marker lights, Marathon style headliner, and jump seats rounded out the package. Half the cabs were ordered with air conditioning. The yellow, Dupont Centari 218, was accompanied by top and bottom checkerboard stripes with no roof lamp or even the holes to mount one. They all came with the only engine available for a 1981 E model, the 267ci inch Chevrolet V8. As of 2003, the news was good and bad. The good news was that there were about 96 Checkers registered in Sweden with most being rare long

wheelbase, A11E models. The bad was that 60 of them were rotten, beat up, no longer in service and 30 were completely gone. During the 1990s, many Swedish punk rockers drove used Checker cabs that were generally in very poor condition from lack of maintenance and people dancing on the hoods and roofs.

In the State of Ohio, every major city had at least one taxi fleet with Checkers and Toledo, Ohio was no exception. In 1982, the Black and White Cab Company went out and purchased 4 final cabs from Checker Motors, all with the 229ci Chevrolet gasoline V6 and, like the other Northern Ohio cab companies during this time period, skipped the air conditioning. They operated Checkers until 1988 when the last of their running, Checker fleet was sold to another cab company in Texas.

Minnesota is famous for its many lakes, but it also had a lot of Checkers once upon a time. Minneapolis and Rochester, home of the Mayo Clinic are just two examples of cities that used to run sizable Checker fleets. The Minneapolis Yellow Cab Company used to operate out of a multi-storey building at 127 1st Avenue N E near downtown, where they worked on cabs and stored Checker parts. Yellow even went so far as to cut one of their Checkers into a pickup truck using the bulletproof partition as the back of the passenger compartment. They used it to make parts runs.

Above: a nice example of the ubiquitous Chicago red and white was this 1981 or 1982 Lakeside cab waiting in the Chicago O'Hare cab pool in 1984. There were at least 5 possible red and white two-tone combinations in Chicago alone. Sporting a bulletproof partition and air conditioning, as many Chicago Checker cabs did, it was ready to make the driver some fundage. Under the hood, the ubiquitous 229ci Chevrolet V6 was powered by gasoline. It seems that only the Chicago Checkers and Yellows had the factory propane option in that service area.

Below: the lower level at Chicago O'Hare Airport still offered a healthy dose of purpose-built taxis as late as 1984. At the head of the line is a green and ivory of 1980 to 1982 vintage. Chicago Checker Cab was and still is the only Chicago cab operator allowed to use checkerboard stripes on their taxicabs. Like its fellow Yellows, these cabs had the Rear Seat Forward option with air conditioning. Like most of the 1982 Yellows, all of the approximately 250 1982 Chicago Checker Cab Checkers came equipped with the factory propane set up mated to the 229ci Chevrolet V6. Many Chicago Checker propanes were retired after only three years' of service.

Above: circa 1984, this 1979 LWB A11E State cab was turning off of Michigan Avenue and into the past as it was about to have its fifth birthday, which meant it was about to be too old to work in Chicago. The State Cab Company had a few of these large cabs and bought their last one in 1981. It is the standard Chicago two-tone blue combination. Front bumper guards and rear chrome stone shields added some bling. State Cab ordered interiors in red vinyl, a fairly rare colour in the jumbo. Powering this husky cab was the required Chevrolet 305ci V8 with a 2-barrel carb. The 350ci 4-barrel V8 option was rarely ordered in any Checker back in 1979.

Below: another example of the Chicago two-tone blue combination was this 1979 Robertson cab, pulling into O'Hare airport around 1984. Robertson was a family owned cab company and once had about 19 Checkers in its fleet. Their last new Checker purchases were for two A11s in 1982. The hand painted lettering on the rear doors was nicely done. Robertson typically went for the grey vinyl interiors with the standard back seat but skipped the jump seats and the air conditioning. The Robertson Cab Company no longer operates, but the family currently is in the limousine business.

Above: a 1982 Model A11 sits at Lexington, Kentucky's United Garage awaiting the next shift. It was ordered with the factory propane option to take advantage of the cab company's bulk propane prices. Older Wildcat Cabs had paw prints on them but such whimsies were left off of the newer models for some reason. Several of these Wildcat Cabs were sold in 1988 to the Owl Cab Company in Bend, Oregon for further use. The operator of Owl Cab reported that it cost more to ship the cabs than to buy them. After some more years of service, the ex-Wildcat Checkers were spent and faded away.

Below: most Checker taxis were yellow, but some cab companies like to set themselves apart from the crowd with a distinctive duo- or tri-tone paint scheme as Norfolk Checker Cab did with this 1981 Model A11, wearing paint scheme #135, parked outside of their 1987 garage location on Sewell's Point Road. Their motto on the rear door, "Life is fragile, handle with care", was a nice touch. Norfolk Checker bought their last Checkers in 1982, although didn't order any with jump seats. However, a few were equipped with partitions. All had the Chevrolet 229ci gasoline V6. Old Number 37 was eventually sold, painted orange, and disappeared to Illinois. Norfolk Checker still uses the green, white, and tan colour combination today.

Irving Schlaifer

One of the most recognizable Checkers to ply the streets of DC was this 1981 A11E jumbo belonging to independent operator and head of the Washington DC Taxicab Association, Irving Schlaifer. Mr Schlaifer had been driving white Checkers since buying his first, a white 1958 A9L, from Checker Motors Sales Corporation at 315 West 68th Street in New York City for $2,489. The cab he traded in for this 1981 A11E was an identical white 1977 model. Amazingly, air conditioning wasn't ordered and wasn't required yet in a town known for hot, humid summers. However, Mr Schlaifer did install 9 police-style dome lights in the ceiling of his cab, so that at night, you could read a map or a brochure without trouble, because the original Checker dome lights were not very bright.

Irving Schlaifer had been driving a cab in Washington DC since 1947. His first cab was a 1947 Plymouth, which he kept until trading it for a new 1958 Checker. His speciality was guided tours of the city and for that, the A11E Checker was a good choice for him as it could handle up to 8 passengers. At the time this was a task no other stock sedan, except for the Cadillac limousine could match. Mr Schlaifer's other job, as head of the Washington DC Taxicab Association, was to occasionally lead strikes and protests with his cab. A proponent of the zone system for taxi fares, he constantly went to Capitol Hill to discuss the fare debate and taxi driver's grievances. Mr Schlaifer passed away in 1990 but his last Checker is still around.

Above: the Ritz Cab Company was formed in 1932, and by the time this picture was taken at Stapleton Airport in 1985 it had 32 taxis like this pretty, late model A11 waiting in the cab line. Ritz was purchased by the Metro Cab Company shortly after. Whether it was born with this paint scheme or if it was a white cab painted the butterscotch two-tone by the cab company is unknown at this time, but since the Chevrolet ahead of it was a Ritz with the same colours, the latter is probably the case. The big Checker dealers normally kept a few all-white Model A11s in stock, because not only did certain cab and transit companies use white cars, it was a colour that the public could live with because, when unadorned with taxi signage, a plain, white Checker looks more like a 1958 Chevrolet to most people and not an in-service taxi that a creepy stranger might try and get into at a traffic light.

Below: aside from Denver Yellow Cab's Checker fleet, Zone Cab ran a batch of these remarkable black and white units and this 1981 or 1982 was caught in the taxi line at Stapleton Airport circa 1985. Painted Checker paint pattern #195, the checkerboard along the roof was coloured all black by a special factory order for a different look. Zone, like Yellow, opted for the Rear Seat Forward option with grey vinyl interior, so there was no room for jump seats. A 229ci gasoline Chevy V6 was found under the hood and air conditioning was not included on the extras list when Zone ordered its final ten cabs from Colorado Checker Sales at 3455 Ringsby Court, Denver in 1982. Note how the Ritz Chevrolet Impala cab behind it is wearing a Checker hubcap.

Above: Checkers were popular in Aspen because they could handle a family of four and their ski equipment. Plus, with decent winter tyres, the Checkers were pretty good in snowy conditions. High Mountain Taxi ran a varied fleet of Checkers, some white like this 1976 or 1977 Model A11 and some were orange like the Jeep Wagoneer behind it. The huge roof rack is black and not easy to spot. Virtually all of Aspen cabs were bought second-hand from larger city's fleets. High Mountain, like Mellow Yellow also purchased some used private Marathons to turn into taxis.

Below: it might have been well below zero at the Minneapolis-St Paul Airport during the winter of 1984 but the Checkers were present and accounted for as evidenced by this frosty, 1981 Minneapolis Yellow Cab. Yellow was a regular buyer of ex-Chicago Yellow Cabs and there is no record of them ordering any new Checkers in 1982. Yellow Cab #76 is following black Skybird Cab #477. The intense salt treatment used to melt ice on the roads wreaked havoc on the Checker bodies.

Checker - the All-American Taxi

Above: the woman in the striped red shirt is the driver of this Bahamian taxi, which was a customized 1980 Model A11E jumbo from Fort Lauderdale dealer Southeast Checker Sales, on Federal Highway. Typical for nearly all non-Freeport Taxi Checkers, the word "taxi" was hand painted discreetly on the front doors in an almost Gothic style. Between the alloy wheels, custom paint job, landau top, chrome accents and opera windows, this was a regal looking taxi. Southeast built several hundred A11 and A11E customs each year, except for 1982, although the short wheelbase units far outnumbered the long ones. The vinyl tops were problematic in the Bahamas because the ocean mist would get under the vinyl and start making rust bubbles.

Below: this 1979 Model A11E Freeport Taxi had a trunk so packed that it must have taken an experienced driver to put it together without losing a bag or two on each turn! Most 1979 E models had the standard 305ci Chevrolet V8 but a few, mostly private Marathons, opted for the 350ci Chevrolet V8. On the island, speed was not that important so the Checkers used that extra grunt to haul car loads of cruise ship patrons and their accoutrements to and from the hotels. When this picture was taken in 1986, the Checker fleet at Freeport Taxi was slowly turning into a Chevrolet Station Wagon fleet as the older Checkers, like this hard-working example became too old and uneconomical to repair.

Above: like a red, red, rose, this 1976 or 1977 A11E jumbo was likely an ex-Freeport Taxi that the new owner had to paint another colour so it couldn't be confused with an in-service Freeport Taxi. In painting it red, they painted not only the body, bumpers, grille etc, but they even painted over the rear quarter windows in an attempt to create a more formal cab. We get a better view of the hand painted "taxi" logo that was found on nearly all Bahamian taxis. Being the jumbo model, it probably had the standard 305ci Chevrolet V8, unless it was originally built for California, which only certified the 350ci Chevrolet V8 as being smog compliant.

Below: a New Yorker visiting Stockholm in 1994 might have been pleasantly surprised to see this pretty yellow and black Checker sitting at the curb. Being a 1981 long wheelbase jumbo, it must have been one of the last batch ordered by Kjellberg Invest Ab, as there were no 1982 Checkers registered in Sweden circa 2003. In addition to the cosmetic changes that Checker had to do for export purposes, they were required to add a front stabilizer bar to each Checker by special order SL 282. For the snow, the Trac-Loc rear end and under seat heater were other "must haves" on the order wish list. The jump seats, which gave the cab up to nine-passenger capacity, were pretty much an obvious option on the bigger body. (Lars Wennerqvist)

9
The Last Years of Checker Sedans and Special Variants in Service

On February 22 1982, two nearly identical Checkers, with serial numbers only two digits apart were built for vastly different municipal purposes in sharply contrasting environments. Laketran, which provides transportation for Lake County, Ohio ordered this single unit to augment its fleet of buses. Laketran checked off the optional 267ci Chevrolet V8, air conditioning, grey vinyl upholstery and jump seats, plus a 105-amp alternator and Trac-Loc rear axle to cope with Northern Ohio's heavy snowfall. The car was in service for about ten years and stored for another five before being auctioned off around 2007. The other, for Florida's Monroe County Sheriff Department can be seen on page 151.

Whilst the Checker's legacy is as an iconic taxicab, several hundred cars were sold each year to private owners and commercial interests, who were aware of the fact that the only other production sedan with this much interior room was the expensive and relatively complex Cadillac Fleetwood 75 limousine. Since Checkers were virtually hand built in very small numbers, the factory was able to customize their product line to suit a customer's needs in terms of paint, interior configuration and special equipment or deletions. For example, if a buyer wanted to use an A11 or A11E as the basis for a package delivery car, they could specify the SL267 delete which got rid of the entire rear seat, whilst an additional option, the SL629, did away with

the rear seat belts as well. Since Checker made almost all of their own interiors, special order upholstery and split seat cushions were not out of the realm of possibility.

Checker Motors suggested many uses for their cars other than taxi service and they regularly spelled it all out in their brochures. One such brochure listed the A12E Marathon long wheel-base sedan as "the perfect car for VIP pick up and delivery, municipal and local government officials, livery, corporations, resorts and hotels, schools, funeral directors, religious institutions". Additional uses included law enforcement, military, senior transport, crew transit, medical, rail inspection, security, mail, fire, ranch, and island jitney service.

The Last Years of Checker Sedans and Special Variants in Service

Probably the most unlikely and little known non-taxi use of a Checker was by the US State Department, who routinely offered US diplomats the option of a Cadillac or a Checker when on assignment in foreign lands. The Marathon's high ground clearance and dated styling was sometimes better for countries with poor roads and impressionable locals, since a sedan with 1950s styling didn't scream wealth and could pass for a Russian car. This 1962 State Department A12 Marathon looked bone stock on the outside, but inside it was laid out like a limousine, with a broadcloth rear seat, privacy partition and a black vinyl front seat. Convenience items included air conditioning, power windows, power steering and brakes. Power was from the fairly rare 226ci Continental Red Seal OHV six. These cars were placed in service all around the world. For example, in 1964 the US Envoy to Vietnam, Henry Cabot Lodge was spotted riding around Saigon in a black Checker Marathon sedan that had special pistol compartments built into the rear doors. In the early 1960s, the Ambassador to the Court of St James in London used a 1961 Checker Marathon as his private ride because it was the only American car with enough room for the top hat he was required to wear. The British number plate, "USA 1" bespoke his position as did the white, oval Corps Diplomatique plate mounted just above it, which came in very handy for avoiding parking tickets.

The rear compartment of this State Department Marathon was quite livable with comfy, broadcloth upholstery, a nice folding armrest, and thicker-than-normal carpeting on that famous, almost flat Checker rear floor. The power window switches were built into the ashtray areas. A music radio was tucked into the area just above where the armrest folds into the rear cushion, so that pampered passengers could listen in on unfolding events. The odd, single jump seat facing the right rear door was probably for security personnel. The Checkers ordered by the State Department varied in colour and equipment, with some featuring front metal sunroofs and white steering wheels for use on desert assignments. The Checker State Department cars were replaced during the 1970s, mostly by Chevy Suburbans.

The long wheelbase sedans were a throwback to the pre-1956 era, when 8-passenger sedans with rectangular jump seats were available for large families or for commercial operators like hotels or airport service providers, where a bus was too big and a stock sedan too small. During the 1980s, the Harley Hotel chain had a string of hotels across the Northern Ohio area and between 1979 and 1980 each one was treated to a new, nine passenger Checker Marathon A12E. The suggested retail price of a new 1980 A12E model began at $9,653, about $1,000 more than the regular wheelbase Marathon A12. Ordered originally in white with black vinyl roofs and blue vinyl upholstery, the fleet was repainted in the mid-1980s with their tops dyed white and horizontal blue stripes along the sides. These jumbos were in service for another year or two before they were retired and replaced with vans. Circa 1988, one unlucky Harley Hotel Checker, driven by a Harley maintenance man, wound up in a demolition derby at the Berea, Ohio County Fair- not a very dignified ending for such a stately car! A photo of it, after the race, can be seen on page 128.

During the late 1980s Pittsburgh, Pennsylvania had a lot of Checkers running around. Not only with the Yellow Cab Company but others too. For example, Colonial Cab had their green Checkers and Tube City Taxi of McKeesport ran orange ones as evidenced by this 1980 Tube City Airport Limousine parked in front of Pittsburgh Airport circa 1985. This jumbo A11E is a rare beast in its own right, but Number 22 was one of approximately 13 ordered with the notorious 350ci Oldsmobile Diesel V8 engine. It was a good concept but initial examples were not reliable. The fleet was converted to gasoline Oldsmobile 350ci V8s because the Chevrolet 350ci V8 wouldn't bolt up to the Oldsmobile 400 transmissions already in the vehicles. All the orange Checkers were retired by 1988. A photo of their fate can be found on page 138.

It is no secret that Checker Motors had a major presence in the New York City area and there wasn't a place you could go where you wouldn't see a Checker of some sort operating. Anybody who either lived on Long Island or regularly spent time in LaGuardia or Kennedy airports during the 1980s will remember the blue Long Island Airports Limousine Checkers (LIALS for short), passing through on their seemingly ceaseless journey to pick up and drop off passengers. The LIALS Checker fleet consisted of 12- and 15-passenger 8-door Aerobuses and 9-passenger A11Es, which supplemented their large city buses. The Checkers were ordered and picked up at the dealer in Long Island City and a picture of two, brand new, 1980 LIALS cars be seen on page 91. While the dealer installed the New York-style strap iron bumper guards, LIALS bolted huge roof racks to holes drilled through the B and C door posts. LIALS was also known to seek out used jumbo A12E and A11E trade-ins from the dealer to paint blue and put into service. These hard working cars had front air conditioning, grey vinyl upholstery and also two-way radios, so they could facilitate passenger pickups and drop-offs along Long Island's busy freeways.

It's a pity that Checker didn't build any hearses, as there were funeral directors who might have bought a couple, as evidenced by these two 1981 Marathon funeral cars used by the R H Greene Funeral Home in Warrenton, North Carolina. Equipped with the 229ci Chevrolet V6 and air conditioning, these cars had the traditional "R H Greene" funeral signs mounted on the inside of the rear doors. Both of the low mileage cars were retired and sold in the 1990s. It is curious that R H Greene didn't opt for the longer, more formal Checker Marathon A12E models. (R H Greene)

Checker - the All-American Taxi

The use of automobiles as railcars has been around almost as long as the car itself, but this really came into its own during the 1940s, when the Fairmont Railway Motors company came out with a line of bolt-on, adjustable railroad wheels that could adapt ordinary cars and trucks to run on railroad tracks. These converted units, known as Highway-Rail Vehicles, or Hi-Rails for short, could be raised or lowered and used the vehicle's original rubber wheels for traction and braking. While being handy for jobs like track maintenance, inspection, and repair, they were also a great way to move workers and equipment to remote construction sites where there were no roads. When one of these unusual cars was in service and on the rails, they were said to be in "engineering possession" of the tracks and no other traffic was allowed. Pictured is a brand new 1964 Checker Marathon station wagon with a recently installed Hi-Rail system. This wagon is so new that it still has Checker's window sticker in the left rear window! Being an early 1964, it still had the 226ci OHV Continental Red Seal six under the bonnet and, being a working car, the transmission was probably the standard three-speed manual on the column. A left hand spotlight, radio, and roof rack were conspicuous options. Checkers destined for rail car conversions were referred to as "custom jobs" by the factory because they required special springs and had some specific suspension parts needs. Hi-Rail type conversions are still available today, but seem to be limited only to trucks.

Before the advent of modern electronics, news bureaux had to rely on their roving reporters in order to be kept abreast of the latest newsworthy events. In 1965, station WKLZ, 1470AM in Checker's hometown of Kalamazoo, Michigan bought three A12 Marathons directly from the factory to use as radio news cars. While little is known about the trio, they were probably equipped with the very popular 230ci Chevrolet six and automatic transmission combination. WKLZ spent about $2700 for the base Marathon and then opted for the pretty two-tone paint, which ran out at $23.56, full wheel covers at $15.66, and the Borg-Warner automatic transmission for $242.51. If they ordered the power steering and brakes, that would have added $74.39 and $41.11 respectively to the final tab. By buying directly from the factory, WKLZ saved on three shipping charges. Transactions of this nature occurred at the Checker Sales building just behind the factory.

When Checker introduced the 1960 station wagon line, its relatively compact exterior dimensions and large interior room motivated at least one business, The American Tobacco Company to order up a fleet of cute sedan delivery vans for merchandise delivery purposes. The rear seat was deleted, the rear quarter windows replaced with steel panels and the rear tailgate glass wore the optional Aerobus steel protective straps. To promote its products, American Tobacco had small ad carriers placed on the rear quarter panels, and in a nice touch, the company's name was spelled out in chrome script on the front wings for all to see.

The interior of the American Tobacco Company panel van. The number of sedan deliveries built is unknown, but it's too bad that Checker didn't make a regular model out of it; most sedan deliveries have only two doors, which means that the driver has to reach behind the front seat to grab items near the front of the cargo area.

The Checker Adaptomobile was a flexible vehicle for its time. Interestingly, the wheelchair was upholstered in the same material that Checker put in the A8, indicating that this was probably all done in-house at the factory. With the wheelchair locked down as shown, there was still room for three adults in the back seat, as well as headroom for the wheelchair occupant. Checker would cater to the handicapped all the way to the end of production in 1982 with special order 180-degree rear door hinges, floor pockets for wheelchairs, removable front passenger seats, and split rear seat cushions. It was not unusual for pre-1970 cab companies to have had at least one wheelchair accessible Checker in a fleet for specialized runs. That job today is handled by vans. With the addition of some ramps stored in the trunk, a special wheelchair could be wheeled into the A8 by tilting the driver's seat up and removing one or both of the rear seat cushions. Production numbers for the Adaptomobiles were probably very low.

Until 1954, the last moderately-priced American sedans with enough room for a patient on a stretcher were the same contenders that were approved for taxi use in New York City, namely Checker and Chrysler. Previously, for small towns and hamlets that couldn't afford a real ambulance, large sedans could be converted to allow for a stretcher by removing the front passenger seat and sometimes making the right side B-post removable for easier loading. It was also not unusual to have rear doors with special 180-degree hinges. After the end of Chrysler's long wheelbase sedan line in 1954, Checker was left as the last viable sedan-based ambulance option in the US. Shown here is a Checker A8 model that was one of a fleet of at least ten cars purchased by the Brooklyn, New York chapter of the American Red Cross. Their use is currently unknown but it is very possible that they were set up for staff transport as well as possible patient transfers by utilizing removable front passenger seats and split rear seat cushions. The licence plates indicate that these A8s were not registered as for hire vehicles.

Above: some cab companies with lots of Checkers, like Denver Yellow Cab tended to use them for everything from push cars to courtesy vehicles, since they already had shelves of parts to service them. The Supervisor at Denver Yellow was lucky enough to drive this white late-70s A11E jumbo sedan around and his ride was spotted at Denver's Stapleton Airport around 1985. The car was embellished with chrome gravel shields on the rear fenders, a $48 option, and additional "Mickey Mouse" stoplights mounted on the top quarter area of the trunk lid, just like the rest of the Denver Yellows. Presumably this was meant to reduce rear end collisions before the federally mandated high-mounted stop light requirement of 1986. It probably had the standard 305ci Chevrolet V8, since the 350ci V8 was on the way out for fuel economy reasons. By 1980, the 350ci V8 was no longer on the option list. The 305ci V8 soon followed it, leaving the 267ci Chevrolet V8 as the only power for the jumbo sedans by the end of production.

Below: in the 1960s, Puerto Rico had a jitney service between towns, where all manner of conveyances would come by and, for a modest charge, carry you down the road. The Checker Motors executive in charge of exports, Max Hickox, regularly sent A11E jumbos to the Checker dealer in San Juan for jitney service. He would have them painted up in all sorts of bright, electric colours, presumably for visibility's sake. This Checker jitney probably had, at the very least, a Chevrolet 230ci straight six under the bonnet, combined with the Borg Warner automatic transmission, which was a good combination for the rough life that was coming. This 1968 A11E Puerto Rico-bound jumbo had rubber mat flooring, a suspended vinyl headliner like a Marathon. An optional chrome rear passenger grab handle that went between the B posts precluded the use of headrests. Oddly, this car was also ordered with the chromed footrest from the formal Checker limousine, which demonstrates how Checker Motors would build a car pretty much the way you wanted it.

The Last Years of Checker Sedans and Special Variants in Service

While Checkers were used for handicapped and non-life threatening transport in the US, some Europeans took the matter much further by using the Checker as a basis for some interesting ambulances and hearses. The 1965s shown here in Switzerland probably began life as knockdown export kits using a standard Checker front cowl on a 6 door Aerobus chassis with no rear body. These were usually accompanied by a wooden crate, lashed to the chassis, with Checker trinkets like hubcaps and trim pieces inside. A spare wheel would normally accompany the crate. Then the bodies were entirely fabricated by a Swiss coachbuilder from the end of the front wings to the tip of the rear bumper for service in Zurich. The standard engine used in all Aerobuses circa 1965 was the 327ci Chevrolet V8, coupled to a three speed manual transmission. Power steering and brakes were also standard Aerobus issue but a Borg-Warner automatic transmission would cost you nearly $250 more. Remarkably, one of these 1965 Checker ambulances survives today. The last European Checker ambulances are thought to have been built around 1969.

10
Checkers Phased Out

The New York State town of Canandaigua, situated in the scenic, Finger Lakes region used pale yellow Checker A11s in their transit system until the late 1980s. Shown is one of approximately six 1978 models that eventually wound up at Crystal Auto Parts in Canandaigua after being retired. The cars all had the 250ci Chevrolet straight six motor and red interiors with round jump seats. Like many eastern Checkers, they had gotten a little rusty and as demand for them as used cars was practically zilch, they went to the recycling yard as a group. This mass junking of Checkers, or any brand of cab was not and isn't an unusual event. When the new vehicles are expected in, operators have to do what they have to do to make room for the fresh faces. With the Checkers, once they were phased out of a fleet, the specialized parts for them frequently became so-much-a-pound because everybody else was disposing of their parts, too. Some older cab companies are still finding Checker bits and pieces decades after the boxy cabs themselves have gone away.

Up until the late 1980s, it was a common practice for businesses using Checkers to retire them onto a trash-strewn back lot where they could be scavenged for parts in order to keep the newer cars going. For example, a 1976 door, bumper, grille, fender, trunk lid, or windshield would fit a 1982 model. This interchangeability of parts between model years made Checker a truly recyclable car and was one of the reasons that some fleet buyers stuck with them in the

first place. Normally, by the time most operators were done picking the good stuff off of the parts cars, very little was left beyond a bare shell, and the number of actual ex-working Checkers that survived this dismemberment process is extremely small. It was only when the last cars were retired that many whole cabs were junked or sold off because they no longer had a reason to exist.

When the Checker assembly line went down

Checker's hometown had a few cab companies that actually used the local product and the Kalamazoo Yellow Cab Company, located at 847 Portage Avenue was one of them. Many of its cabs were 1981 ex-Chicago Yellow Cabs that had been refurbished by the Checker factory in the mid-1980s for them. Checker Motors would only refurbish worn-out but still operational fleet cabs by running them through the factory again, replacing all the outer sheet metal and doing some minor mechanical work. Non-functioning cabs were generally not eligible for this overhaul process. The back lot at Kalamazoo Yellow Cab in 1987 had over a dozen cars like Number 41, a retired 1976 A11 that were part way through a recycling process, although a major class trumpet vine seemed intent on keeping Old Number 41 for itself. Ultimately, the vine didn't win, as the cab company ceased operations in 1988 and the Checker fleet was sold off or junked. At that time, running Checkers were priced at $150 apiece and the dead ones were $75. What was left of Number 41 was scrapped at a nearby junkyard when the cab company building was turned into a furniture store. The last Kalamazoo Yellow Cab Checker in service was Number 50, a 1981, which was donated to a local museum that left it out in the elements to rot.

on July 12, 1982 and there were no more new Checkers, a lot of cab companies were faced with the novel and, for some, intimidating task of choosing a new taxi brand for the first time in decades. It didn't take long for the once-ubiquitous Checker cab to become a minority at taxi stands in places that they used to dominate, like Chicago, Illinois or Norfolk, Virginia. By 1988, nearly all the commercially used Checkers were quietly retired nationwide for a variety of reasons, mostly that the cars were worn out, depreciated on the books, and some cities had age restrictions on for-hire vehicles, usually five years that forced all cabs, regardless of condition or make, off the streets upon reaching a certain age. Sadly, as the sixty-year reign of the Checker ended and the final cabs got gamey from harsh service, many drivers avoided taking them out at all and some companies had to offer a lower, daily lease rate on the Checkers than the newer, Brand X cabs in an attempt to generate some driver interest in the old taxi gold. To make matters worse, spare parts began to get spotty and its status as an orphan brand scared a lot of possible, secondary operators away. By 1990, nearly all the Checkers were gone.

Above: this pair of retired mid-seventies Mellow Yellow taxis from Aspen, Colorado seem to have been swallowed by an advancing glacier in the winter of 1984, but given up again by May 1985, when their picture was taken. The back lot at Mellow Yellow had at least 15 Checkers in various conditions, hanging out with a couple of Jeep Wagoneer taxis and a scruffy 1970 Cadillac Fleetwood 75. The Checkers, when equipped with snow tyres and a little bit of weight in the rear were pretty good in the white stuff and hauled many a skier from Aspen to the ski areas and back, using large roof racks to handle the bulky skis and poles. The placement of the "Yellow" taxi dome on the roof rack is a bit whimsical, but it was wired and functional. Many of the Mellow Yellow Cabs were purchased used from some of the numerous Colorado cab companies that used Checkers at that time, although a few were ex-civilian Marathons painted yellow. As the 1980s progressed and the classic cabs became rusty and harder to maintain, the Checkers were gradually replaced with more modern, four wheel drive conveyances and today there is nary a trace that Aspen was ever a Checker hot-spot.

Below: it might look like this couple of rare A11E taxis were rusting away in the Northeast USA, but they were actually decomposing about 50 miles west of Stockholm, Sweden in 1997. The Checker dealer in Stockholm, Kjellberg Invest Ab, had been ordering jumbo A11Es from the factory expressly for taxi service in Sweden and, while they were very similar to those sold in the States, differences included a speedometer in kilometres, the changing of the round, rear side marker lights from red to amber, the deletion of all seat belts and the addition of a front suspension stabilizer. The colour used, Yellow #218 was accompanied by top and bottom checkerboards and optional "Checker" script for the front wings and boot lid. To handle the snowy winters the Trac-Loc rear axle, under-seat heater and rear defogger were checked on the order form. Kjellberg Invest Ab ordered less than ten of these cabs in 1981 and none in 1982. After taxi service, most of these Checkers were pretty rusty and many wound up being abused by Swedish punk rockers during the 1990s.

Above: black and white wasn't the most popular paint combination on a Checker but a steady stream of buyers chose it and each seemed to use it differently. The Black and White Cab Company of Toledo, Ohio had an attractive fleet using Checker Motors paint pattern #168, which, interestingly, had the grille painted black instead of the regular dull silver colour. They purchased their four last Checkers in 1982 and all had the 229ci Chevrolet gasoline V6, red interior with jump seats and no air conditioning. The 229-cube motor wasn't thought of very well at Toledo Black and White, because they found themselves replacing the engines after only 90,000 miles. They preferred the longevity and simplicity of the 250ci Chevrolet straight six motors which Checker stopped using later in 1979. By the end of 1988, the last Toledo Black and White Checkers were retired and all got the axe except for a 1982 model, Number 222, which was stuffed with parts and driven to Texas by a cab operator. Shown is retired Number 206, a 1980 model that has had its back axle removed for use in one of the company's other, still operating Checkers, since a 1980 differential sported the same 2:72 ratio that the 1978 to 1982 models.

Below: a rare sight indeed was found in at the back lot at Freeport Taxi on Grand Bahamas island, circa 1988, where the rarest late model Checker taxis, the jumbo A11E models were lined up for recycling as if they were common Chevrolets. The colourful fleet consisted of 1979 to 1982 A11Es and most were purchased new and delivered through the Freeport Taxi Company, which was, coincidentally, the Checker dealer for the Bahamas. The last twelve 1982 A11Es were ordered six at a time and trucked to Dania, Florida for export. Freeport Taxi parts cars were very important to keep the fleet alive, because they were not only on an island but also in a foreign country. When Checker parts became harder to get in the mid-1980s, Freeport Taxi was known to buy out cab companies' parts inventories on the mainland US and ship the spares to Freeport. The last 2 Freeport Checkers were retired on October 31 1991. All the Freeport Checkers but one, Number 19, were ultimately crushed on the island and put on a barge for a Miami scrap facility.

For cab companies, it is risky to sell a used cab that looks like it might be in service, because it might confuse the public or worse, get the cab company in trouble if it is used in a nefarious way. Cleveland, Ohio's United Garage handled that problem by painting their retired cabs mostly black before selling them, a practice that they had been doing since the early 1960s. If you lived in Cleveland in 1965, you could buy a running retired cab, painted entirely black, with a flathead engine and three speed floor shift for only $25. By 1988, the price had skyrocketed up to $300 for a single unit, but could drop as low as $50 apiece if multiple cars were purchased. After selling several to a local monastery, United Garage donated at least four more to the organization, but only after General Manager, Bill Klug, queried the Brothers as to what they were going to do with all those Checkers. Here is an example of one such car, a 1982 ex-Cleveland Yellow cab with the 229ci Chevrolet gasoline V6, no air conditioning, a black interior and only one jump seat. To add to the risk of selling an unpainted Checker locally, another possible headache for a cab company was the unwanted return of a past buyer who was looking to mooch some specialized, Checker-only items from the operator's parts bin.

Since the Checker has the undeserved reputation for being built like a tank, a lot of dreamers assumed that they could win a demolition derby with one, as evidenced by this once-pretty 1980 Marathon A12E, which now looked like Death sucking on a Lifesaver! It had been a proud member of the Berea, Ohio Harley Hotel fleet, but as the hotel chain went to vans in the mid-1980s, the hapless Checker jumbo was demoted from hauling guests to schlepping food around the grounds. After that, it was ushered into the 1988 Berea, Ohio County Fairgrounds demolition derby by a Harley Hotel maintenance man. What most folks don't seem to notice is that the radiator is only a few inches behind the grille on a Checker, so the first time the front end gets punched, the radiator will lose coolant and the car will overhead, putting it out of the race. Although derby Checker number 116 put up a good fight, it did not win. A sad ending indeed for a car that cost the hotel chain about $11,000 when new.

The US Military had been a steady buyer of Checker sedans and airport limousines since at least the early 1960s. Every branch, whether it was the Air Force, Army, Navy or Department of Defense got to order some up in their own colours and equipment, mostly for troop transport around and between bases. While it may seem bizarre today, the military actually sent inspectors to Checker Motors in Kalamazoo to observe their Aerobuses being built, presumably to make sure that all the bolts were put in properly and all the torques were correct. Aerobuses were built by a team of about six men over in Plant One and their production was completely separate from the taxi-Marathon assembly line. Two buses a day was the normal output. This olive drab 1973 ex-Army bus was spotted languishing on the back lot of a Midwestern sewage treatment plant in 1987. 1973 was one of the last years that the military would order from Checker, as the American van had improved to the point where they began to make more sense than what were, essentially, custom built eight door station wagons with specialized parts requirements.

BUS, MOTOR, 12 PASS., STATION WAGON TYPE, 4 X 2				
MANUFACTURED BY CHECKER MOTORS CORP. MODEL A-12W8M				
KALAMAZOO, MICHIGAN U.S.A.				
MFG. SERIAL No.	9782-53518	FSN No.	23V3-100371	
VEHICLE CURB WEIGHT			POUNDS	
PAYLOAD, MAXIMUM			POUNDS	
GROSS WEIGHT, MAXIMUM			POUNDS	
DATE OF DELIVERY	10/73	CONTRACT No.	GS-00S-2296	
REG. NO.	00-1821	U.S. PROPERTY	WARRANTY 12 MO.	MI.

The factory was required to put this metal plate on the dashboards, as per government regulation, identifying the bus as US Property with specifications listed such as the manufacturer, 5,305lb curb weight and maximum payload weight of 2,375lb, or the approximate weight of twelve, 200lb soldiers. As military Aerobuses were ordered with no music radios, Checker usually placed it where the radio would have gone. Interestingly, this 1973 Army Aerobus identification plate even lists the Checker warranty at 12 months and 12,000 miles!

The vicinity of Long Island City, just over the river from Manhattan was a popular place for cab companies to be located, because real estate there was generally quite a bit cheaper than Manhattan. Lots of fleets ran Checkers out of this area and were supported by the large Checker Motor Sales Corporation dealership just blocks away on 38th Street. Many New York City fleet operators only keep their cabs for two or three years, so most of the Checkers were put out to pasture by 1985 with no place to go. The best ones were sold to other towns for further use, but a vast majority hit the junkyard circuit or ended life as a push car, like this 1981 example spotted in 1992. Push cars were an inexpensive way for cab companies to push dead taxis into the shop for repair and Checkers were popular push cars simply because they had the biggest and best bumpers in town. Some operators even went so far as to bolt a second bumper to the top of the front bumper for maximum pushing area. Our subject cab already had the New York City style strap iron bumper guards so the owner just hung some tyres on them for gentle prodding. The sides of the ex-cab were painted black and "Not for hire" was stencilled on the rear doors twice, because in the tri-state area at that time, many residents regarded nearly every Checker as possibly being for hire and it was not unheard of for folks to step into a private car at a stoplight and demand to be taken somewhere. Most push cars were junked the first time something broke that wasn't easy or cheap to fix.

Above: in a corner of the Hunt Transportation back lot in Omaha, Nebraska, old Checker cab Number 206 knew it was having a bad day when it woke up upside down with its guts ripped out! Shorn of its tyres, drive train, propane tanks and even its bumpers, the next stop for 206 wasn't going to be a pretty place. This 1981 A11 worked for Hunt Transportation under the Checker Cab banner along with two other Hunt cab companies, Yellow and Happy Cab. All the 1981 Hunt Checker Cabs were converted to propane fuel when new, since Checker didn't offer the propane option until 1982. The green and ivory made for a pretty colour combination and the red interiors looked sharp with it. Hunt ordered air conditioning with jump seats in all their Checkers and Number 206 was no exception. The entire Checker fleet was phased out by 1988 and replaced with, mostly, Chevrolet Impalas.

Below: by 1988, the story of these McKeesport, Pennsylvania Tube City Airport Limousines now echoed that of the empty steel tube factory in the background: once nice but now nasty. Not only were the Checker A11E jumbos mechanically wanting from years of use on Pittsburgh's hilly roads, but the winter road salt had been nibbling at them. The rust is clearly visible on Number 7, a 1980 model. The Oldsmobile 350ci diesel V8 was offered in Checkers from 1979 to 1981 as a $2,355 option, and in an unusual move, Tube City had purchased some brand new yellow 1980 A11 diesel taxis from the NYC Checker dealer and painted them all Tube City orange. They and put all of them into service except for one, which was kept inside and never used. With only 22 miles on the odometer, this rare bear was sold in the early 1990s to a buyer in Florida and has not been heard from since. The number of surviving A11 and A11E ex-taxis that still have an Oldsmobile diesel motor under the bonnet is extremely small and could probably be counted on one hand.

Above: like a pair of snowmen melting in springtime, these two 1980 A11E nine passenger sedans sat behind the Checker factory and rusted away during the 1990s. They were originally used by a local college and perhaps they were meant to be resold or possibly restored, as the factory was wont to do in those days, but nothing like that happened, so they just sat outside and slowly degenerated beyond the point of economic repair. When their rockers panels fell on the ground, Checker finally cut them up. During the final years, production of these long wheelbase cabs was normally less than one hundred units per annum. Their prices began at $8,782, about $700 more than a standard A11.

Below: Minneapolis Yellow Cab used to operate a nice fleet of, mostly, Checkers out of a multi-storey building at 127 1st Avenue NE until about 1988. Like most taxi garages, they had a body shop, a mechanical repair area and a corner dedicated to cab disassembly and storage of spare parts. For parts runs, Minneapolis Yellow took one of their better retired 1979 A11s and cut it into a serviceable pick-up truck, using the bulletproof partition as the back of the driver's cab. In addition, the rear doors were sealed shut, thick plywood laid down for the cargo bed floor and aluminium running boards were added to bling it up a bit. When photographed in 1984, the nifty truck was about to schlep a bad transmission to a shop for rebuilding. Like most 1979 Checker A11s, it had the 250ci Chevrolet straight six motor, mated to a GM Turbo 400 transmission. Late 1979s switched to the 229ci Chevrolet V6. Even in the vast GM model line-up, this was the only application for this engine/transmission combination.

Lost and almost forgotten was this 1976 A11 belonging to Norview Cars Inc of Norfolk, Virginia. With stuff piled around it, the cab was probably not accessible when the scrap man came to take the rest of the 1976s away, so it avoided the guillotine just long enough to be unearthed in 1988 when the newer Norview Checkers were disposed of. Old 102 had the ubiquitous 250ci Chevrolet straight six motor, although it now had an integral manifold and head design that proved to be not only prone to cracking when overheated but expensive to replace. GM went back to the separate head and manifold in 1978, probably after getting an earful from disappointed owners. Old 102's list price began at $5,274 and was a pretty colour combination of ivory, white and green using Checker paint pattern #135 with a grey interior. No jump seats were ordered, but the $316 bulletproof partition was, along with front air conditioning, dealer-installed vent shades on the doors and a Cabometer brand taximeter wearing a 1984 inspection sticker. A garage mechanic indicated that this taxi was sidelined with a broken flywheel, which never got repaired. Norview Cars Inc used to order six cabs at a time from the dealer in Long Island City, New York and then have them shipped to Norfolk on one truck.

In 1988, anybody fortunate enough to have had access to the Long Island Airports Limousine Company back lot in Hauppauge, New York was treated to the uncommon vision of nearly a dozen decommissioned eight door Checker Aerobuses scattered around the premises. Ranging in age from the last station wagon models of 1974 to the final 1977 sedan-back versions, most of these rare blue giants had already been partially stripped because a lot of Aerobus parts, like doors, front wings and windshields would fit the newer A11E jumbo cabs that LIALS still had in service. The roof racks were not Checker Motors factory issue but were probably custom crafted for LIALS locally and were held in place by bolts that went through the door posts. Drivers had to be not only skilled enough to manoeuvre these big cars in grinding traffic but strong enough to hoist almost a dozen heavy bags up onto that rack. In an act of naïve optimism, author Ben actually bought one of the 1977 models, number 551 and, after reinstalling some missing parts, nursed it all the way to Ohio without knowing that the frame was broken in three separate places. There were clues however: some doors wouldn't open or close unless the bus was level, the rear window didn't want to stay in and there were some unnerving clanking and clicking noises coming from the undercarriage.

When Columbus, Ohio needed space for their Yellow Radio and Hills fleets in the late Eighties, the retired 1976 to 1979 era Checkers had to go somewhere and most wound up at nearby Buckeye Auto Wrecking. With their drivetrains ripped out, aluminium bumpers scrapped and tyres gone, the next stops for the 71 Checkers and the single Chevrolet Impala were most likely a crusher, then a shredder and a final container trip to the Far East.

11
Checkers Today

This fine 1923 Model H is the oldest surviving Checker taxicab. It now resides at The Gilmore Museum in Hickory Falls, Michigan through the generosity of the Markin Family. It is the epitome of an "assembled car", sporting a generic taxi body produced by The Millspaugh & Irish Corporation and an engine by Buda. Designed for heavy-duty service, Checkers were equipped with all-steel wheels, where most automobiles of the period were equipped with wooden spoke wheels that would never survive the rigours of city taxi service. This Checker was restored by Checker Motors Corporation in the mid 1960s and can be seen in numerous Checker advertisements or brochures (Joe Fay Collection)

The nature of the taxicab and its job means that it is unlikely to survive in any significant numbers for more than the few years for which it is worked. It is a tool to turn a profit, so once it is no longer profitable, it is sent to the scrap yard.

But that doesn't mean that there aren't people who have a nostalgia for old taxicabs, and top of the list for so many of those people is the Checker. The A11 is the one vehicle most people

recognise as an American taxi, and film and TV programme makers still want one, preferably a yellow one when they need to shoot a scene with a taxi in it.

Other people just love them and collect them, but because so many of the older types were scrapped they are extremely rare. There are very many more A11s and A12s around than there are A4s, or A6s. In the following pages are some

Checker - the All-American Taxi

Like the Checker Cab, few examples of Partin-Palmer cars have survived. This Model 20 Roadster is one of them. (Joe Fay collection)

of those old Checkers that have been lovingly restored, or are undergoing restoration.

Great support for owners of old Checkers comes from the Checker Car Club of America, which was formed in April 1982, the year that production of automobiles ceased. The purpose of the club was, and still is to preserve and share photographs, documents, stories and other artefacts related to Checker taxis and automo-biles. Doing great work too is the Checker Cab Group Facebook page, with 400-plus members to date.

The great majority of preserved, and unrestored Checkers are, not surprisingly to be found in the USA, but there are some in the UK and mainland Europe, and there may just be the odd few tucked away in places you'd never expect to find them.

Above, right: one of the few Checker survivors built prior to 1960, This 1931 Model M represents perhaps the most luxurious Checker taxi produced. Designed in a style of "Town Car", taxis of the period were considered luxurious; comparable to Black Cars used today by North American limousine services. The Model M is equipped with "sugar scoop" fenders. A purpose built design, these unique fenders prevent tire damage in case of minor front end "fender benders". The Model M was designed with a closed compartment for passengers with passenger only running boards and driver divider window. Model Ms were equipped with Buda CS6 engines. The Model M depicted in the photo survived via movie car service, appearing in David O Selznik's A Portrait of Jennie (1948) and was a frequent guest star on the Desilu Productions' TV show The Untouchables 1959-1963). The current owner is Charles Curtin of New London, Connecticut. The Curtin family has operated taxis in New London since 1918. (Joe Fay)

Right: when the Checker Model A was introduced in 1940 it had more interior room than any previous Checker produced. It was also the first Checker to migrate away from the limousine concept, towards the "commodity taxi" business. New features were added to enhance the taxi passengers' ride experience, the landaulet top at a touch of a finger, the driver could lower the back section of the roof so passengers could ride in a semi convertible mode. Passengers could open up the ventilator to increase the flow of fresh air, yet still look out of the glass roof for improved sightseeing. Both the glass roof and the landaulet roof were Checker exclusive features and patented by Checker in 1936 and 1939 respectively. The taxi driver also rode with the comfort of Checker exclusive features. The seat was adjustable for driver comfort; Checker claimed that the seat could be adjusted in no less than 15 positions. The exterior design of the Model A has always been the subject of much debate; the airstream styling clearly conflicts with "sugar scoop" fenders. The only known surviving Checker Model A, this 1941 example was sold to a private party in upstate New York. Checker engineer Jim Stout personally delivered the car to the new owners, "breaking the car in" on its drive from Kalamazoo, Michigan to New York. Discovered by Arthur J. Baudendistel in a New York junk yard, Baudendistel restored the vehicle to its current museum quality state. (Joe Fay)

This 1952 A4 served as a New York City taxi, but it was taken out of service in 1953 and parked deep in the woods of Connecticut and left to rot away for over 60 years. One must wonder why an almost new Checker would be abandoned like this, but its current owner found 1950s era beer cans and girlie magazines under the driver's seat! (Mike Riley)

The only known surviving Checker A3 awaits restoration. This rare find originally served as a limo/taxi in Oklahoma City, going on until 1968 to serve a farmer as a family car to haul his eight children. It was then tied up in estate litigation for close to twenty years, eventually finding its way into a Checker collector's hands in 2008. Note the unique sun visor over the windshield. (Mike Riley)

The 1950 Checker Model A4 originally served the taxicab consumers of New York City. On November 15 1956 a California pink slip registration was issued to Loews Inc of Culver City, California, a division of Metro Goldwyn Mayer Pictures. This Checker was used initially for the 1956 MGM picture, A Cater Affair, starring Bette Davis and Ernest Borgnine. One year later it was used in the MGM film, Designing Women, starring Lauren Bacall and Gregory Peck. The MGM prop department made major changes to it, most significant being the addition of a 1953 Hudson Jet Borg-Warner automatic transmission and Jeep CJ steering wheel. It sat in the MGM fleet up until the breakup of the movie company and ultimately sat in a California junk yard until it was rescued by taxi collector Ben Merkel. (Joe Fay)

The only known Model A8 Drivermatic Special, this Checker was ordered by Yellow Cab of Oakland, California and was field tested for potential service. The results of the test were poor, judged as not being able to handle steep San Francisco hills. Yellow Cab executive Bill Rothchild purchased the car when Westgate Corporation took over Yellow in 1962 and he kept the Checker for the next 30 years as his personal transportation. Originally painted navy blue, the car is currently restored in Chicago Checker livery. (Joe Fay)

Above and below: this Checker Model A9 is the oldest surviving A9 known to exist. Production commenced in October 1958 starting with serial number 34000 and this cab carries serial number 34006, so it can be assumed that this car was made on the first day of A9 production. It was originally a New York City taxicab. It then went into second service in Boston, Massachusetts, ending its commercial service in the 1988 movie, Lady in White. Movie car service is a common theme among Checker survivors.

The car is now in pristine condition, but its restoration, done progressively by several Checker collectors uncovered a much rusted body beneath a significant amount of plastic body filler, applied by the movie company prop department. So rotted was the original body that a 1962 Checker Model A12 body was used in the restoration. The resulting "Frankenstein" job retained the chassis, engine, fenders, hood, doors, interior and original steel dashboard. Unique to the A9 when compared to new generation Checkers are the smaller rear fender wheel opening, lower front bumper line with splash pan and special starburst grille. As of 2015, this A9 became the property of Sun Coach Line of McKeesport, Pennsylvania. (Joe Fay)

The ceasing of car production on July 12 1982 was bad news if you were an average customer, because if you asked Checker Motors for a new car to be built after the assembly line quit, the answer was always going to be no. But if you knew Checker president David Markin well enough, you might have sweet-talked a new car out of him, because that's what happened with this 1983 Marathon A12E jumbo that was built in 1983 using a leftover body from years earlier and new parts lying around the factory. A search of the plant didn't turn up any new E model doors, so General Plant Superintendent John Logan suggested using regular rear doors with a filler panel to make up the 9-inch difference in length. Remarkably, Checker assigned this one-off car a 1983 serial number and kept the car's existence a secret for years, because they probably wanted to avoid official scrutiny for building a car without doing the onerous amount of legal paperwork required to sell a new 1983 car in the US. Originally burgundy with a black vinyl roof, this interesting car has been extensively modified by its current owners and now sports gold trim with a custom, white interior and rear sunroof.

The dash of this custom A12E shares the gold plating applied to its external trim.

150

The near twin to the Laketran Checker (page 120) was chosen by Florida's Monroe County Sheriff Department as a lone police unit and was delivered to Southeast Checker Sales in Ft Lauderdale. Like the Laketran car, a 267ci Chevrolet V8, air conditioning, and grey vinyl upholstery were ordered. Where the two Checkers differed the most could be found in the rear compartment; no jump seats were to be found in the sheriff's car. Where some things like its spotlights were a factory installed option, Monroe Country added the special side stripe. This interesting police car served the Key West area for over ten years before being retired. In a strange twist of fate, both the Laketran and Monroe Sheriff's cars wound up only 15 miles apart in Ohio for a short while. Today, the police car lives in Los Angeles and is in the hands of a Checker enthusiast.

Law Enforcement and Security concerns didn't use Checkers much as patrol cars, but the same qualities that made them desirable taxis, like good outward visibility, interior room, and decent manoeuvrability, did trigger the "buy" reaction with some practically-minded sheriffs, especially after the advent of optional V8 power in mid-1964. There was really nothing significantly different between the Checker patrol cars and the cab line, because most of the units were simply Model A11 taxis with V8 power and perhaps a larger alternator for a two-way radio. The Checker dealer in Brookline, Massachusetts sold 4 1981 A11 blue and white police cars for the Chelsea Police Department with the New York fleet package, Code 217, which included frame reinforcements, X-brace on the radiator support and a rod between the two inner front fenders. Unlike its mass produced competitors from Chevrolet, Ford, and Dodge, Checkers already had heavy duty components for taxi service and didn't need to be beefed up for a police beat. That said, most officers weren't too crazy about driving Checker patrol cars, for two major reasons: first of all, they didn't look "macho" enough to suit most officers and secondly, the public didn't always take them seriously. Some folks refused to stop for a squad car that they thought was maybe a 1958 Chevrolet and therefore unlikely to be a current, real cop car. (Joe Pollard)

Above: this 1982 A11, Old Number 98 is a survivor of Norfolk, Virginia Yellow Cab's fleet of 24. Its Chevrolet V6 ran on gasoline, supplied from a pump at the cab company that had this sign overhead: "A thinking fellow drives a Yellow." They were sold off in 1988, at $250 each.

Below: the Black and White Cab Company of Norfolk, Virginia ran these 1982 A11s, with gasoline V6s, doing much work to and from the US Navy base. Old Number 26, one of the final batch delivered has retained its original markings.

Above: not every Checker taxi built in 1982 was put into service, as evidenced by this largely original propane-fuelled A11 that has only managed to amass 2,500 miles in 33 years. Ordered on April 26 1982, built May 28 and delivered behind the Cab Service garage at Checker Motors on July 16, it just made it onto the build roster before Checker stopped taking orders.

Below: in Spring, 1982, as the end of production was near, Checker Motors Sales Corporation management ordered two A11E taxis for conversion into customs; one in grey, pictured here and one in black. Both were fitted with dual air conditioning, rectangular jump seats, larger than normal oval windows, padded tops, American sunroofs and upgraded interiors. The only engine available for the E models was the Chevrolet 267ci V8. Both of these final A11E customs are around today.

Above: Checkers of any sort are a rare sight outside of the USA. This example is actually an A12 Marathon, converted to a taxi. It lives in London. (Olivier Hyafil)

Below: this 1968 Aerobus is still working, at Glacier National Park, Montana. (Bob Hinkley)

Further Reading

Brooklands Road Test Portfolio: "Checker Automobiles". Brooklands Books, 2010
Collection of road tests, magazine reports etc. Pb/ b/w

Georgano, G N: "A History of the London Taxicab". David & Charles, 1972
The first modern generation book on the subject. Long out of print. H/b, b/w

Georgano, G N, Munro, Bill: "The London Taxi". Shire Books, 2009
A pocket history of the subject. P/b, full colour

Hinckley, James: "Checker Cab Co, Photo History" Iconografix, 2003
A comprehensive history of the subject. P/b, b/w

Lemon, Carl: "The Winchester Taxi". Bowden Publishing, 2013
Compact and well researched study of this rare make. P/b, full colour

May, Trevor: "Gondolas and Growlers: The History of the London Horse Cab". Alan Sutton, 1995
An in-depth academic study, but very readable. Now out of print. H/b, b/w

Monier, Chris & Merkel, Ben: The American Taxi: A Century of Service". Iconografix, 2006
A broad history of a very large subject. P/b, colour

Munro, Bill: "FX4 Black Cab Enthusiasts' Manual". Haynes Books, 2012
A comprehensive appraisal of all FX4 and FL2 models. H/b, full colour

Munro, Bill: "London Taxis - a Full History". Earlswood Press, 2014
An in-depth study of the vehicles, from 1897 to 2014. P/b, b/w

Munro, Bill: "Taxi Jubilee - Fifty Years of the Austin FX4 London Taxi". Earlswood Press 2009
A definitive story of this iconic vehicle. P/b, full colour

Scrimger, D L: "Taxicab Scrapbook". Privately published, 1979
Covering a variety of US makes, mostly pre-war. P/b, b/w. Out of print

Rouxel, Claude: "La Grande Histoire des Taxis Français" Edijac, 1989
A definitive history of the subject. French text. H/b, b/w. Out of print

Ward, Rod: "Taxi - Purpose-built Cabs in Britain". Malvern House Publications, 2008
Pictures of cabs of all ages from all around the UK. P/b, b/w with some colour

Warren, Philip, and Linskey, Malcolm: "Taxicabs -A Photographic History". Almark, 1976
Very wide range of photographs, up to the early 1970s. H/b, b/w. Long out of print.

Yost, Stanley K & Bassett, Kathryn: "Taxi! A Look at Checkers Past" Misc. Enterprises,1990
A scrapbook of the make, focussing more on pre-war models. H/b, b/w. Out of print

Earlswood Press

Earlswood Press is an independent UK publishing company, producing illustrated non-fiction books. We specialise in titles relating to the taxi trade, both in London and the rest of the world, but we are expanding our sphere of interest into other transport related topics and books related to the history of London.

Our aim has been to improve the standards within small-scale publishing, and to encourage first-time writers. Thus we work very closely with our authors to ensure that the finished products are as good as they can be.

What to do if you think you have a book we may be interested in publishing

We do not publish fiction, children's books or poetry, because we simply do not have the expertise in these specialist and often highly competitive fields. We currently publish a range of biographies, but for commercial reasons we will no longer be taking on any more.

If you have a transport, motoring history or London-related title you think might interest us, we would like to hear from you. We do expect you to meet certain criteria in sending your submission to us; not because we are being overly fussy, but because altering manuscript and image files to suit the requirements of our typesetting software is time-consuming and thus incurs a cost to us. So, please send your submission in one of two ways:

- By post or email, a SHORT synopsis (say 500-1000 words), a list of chapters, one chapter and some sample illustrations.
- If emailing, please send the text as an attachment in Microsoft Word ONLY. Type it using double spacing in a single, simple font, such as Times, in 12pt and apart from numbering the pages, keep your formatting as simple as possible. DO NOT place your submission in the body of your email.
- If your book is illustrated, send sample illustrations as jpegs or PDFs, attached to your email. DO NOT import any images into the text of a Word document.
- If sending your work by post, print it on one side of A4 paper, using the same formatting rules as for an emailed document, plus some sample illustrations, which should be photocopies at this stage. Please also include return postage to ensure safe return, should we not decide to accept your submission.
- Do make sure you have permission, or can safely secure permission to use any illustrations that are not your property. We do fund the purchase of illustrations from commercial sources, up to a reasonable limit within the budget of the book. Do also ensure that the images you want to include can be sourced in a suitable format. We are happy to advise you on this.

If we feel we can publish your book, we will contact you to discuss how we may proceed.

Earlswood Press

Transport Titles

London Taxis in Camera - a History in Pictures, Old and New - *Bill Munro*

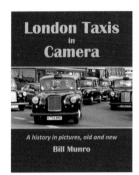

London's taxis have evolved over the years, whilst retaining the essential elements that enable them to perform the job well and be readily identifiable to the travelling public. London Taxis in Camera is the story of those vehicles in pictures, featuring:

 Historical images from across the twentieth century
 Specially shot full colour images of preserved London taxis
 Fascinating snippets of information about the London taxi trade
 A glimpse into the future of the London taxi

100 pages, 246mm x 189mm paperback, full colour, RRP £19.99
ISBN 9780957475458

London Taxis - a Full History *(second edition) - Bill Munro*

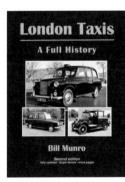

This, the definitive history of London's taxis traces the story of the London taxi from 1897, when the capital's first horseless cab, the Bersey appeared, right up to the present day, featuring:

 The history of every known make, model and prototype
 New information about once-famous names in the industry
 Over 150 photographs, some of which have not been published before
 Technical specifications and production figures

256 pages, 246mm x 189mm paperback, black and white, RRP £17.99
ISBN 9780957475427

Taxi Jubilee - Fifty Years of the Austin FX4 London Taxi - *Bill Munro*

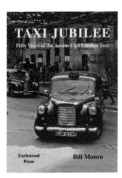

For over fifty years, the FX4 London taxi was a familiar a sight in Britain's capital city. 'Taxi Jubilee' features:

 The story of the FX4 over five decades
 A selection of the special versions ordered by the rich and famous
 Details of many versions sold abroad, other bodies built on its chassis
 Preserved FX4s around the world
 Details of model taxis
 Technical specifications of every major model.

72 pages, 210mm x 146mm paperback, full colour, RRP £7.99
ISBN 9780956230805